A Sip from the Cup of Grace

365 Day Devotional

Vicki Maas

WESTBOW
P R E S S®
A DIVISION OF THOMAS NELSON
& ZONDERVAN

WestBow Press books may be ordered through booksellers or by contacting:

WestBow Press
A Division of Thomas Nelson & Zondervan
1663 Liberty Drive
Bloomington, IN 47403
www.westbowpress.com
1 (866) 928-1240

ISBN: 978-1-5127-6558-8 (sc)
ISBN: 978-1-5127-6559-5 (hc)
ISBN: 978-1-5127-6557-1 (e)

Library of Congress Control Number: 2016919468

Print information available on the last page.

WestBow Press rev. date: 02/01/2017

Introduction

Grace: When God meets our needs not because we deserve it, but simply because of his unconditional love for us.

Unworthiness: When we don't feel good enough to receive God's grace.

How good would we have to be in order to receive God's grace? At what point would we actually feel worthy enough to accept it? If we don't ever get to that point of accepting it, does it mean Jesus wasn't enough? In 2 Corinthians, he tells us that his grace is sufficient for us.

Jesus also said, "Know the truth and the truth will set you free" (John 8:32). Set us free from what? Our sorrow and pain? Our past hurts or fear of the future? Feeling unloved? Selfishness or unkindness? Unforgiveness? Sin of any degree? Can he set us free from our memories of abuse? Everyone has his or her own story or reasons why he or she needs to be set free and allow Jesus into his or her life. Well, almost everyone; some people don't think they need him at all. They don't understand this grace thing. Maybe the fact that you are holding this book in your hands is a sure indicator that you might want to know more about God's goodness. I hope you will accept that he says you are good enough. Don't wait to get all cleaned up before coming to God. He will meet you right where you are. Come, feast at his table. He has a place set just for you!

Lord Jesus, I thank you that it is your plan for the words on these pages to reach all those who seek you. I pray their minds and hearts would be open to all that you have to offer through a daily walk with you. Make their desire to know you more than their belief that there is no other way than depending on themselves. You came to earth to teach and share the love God has so graciously bestowed on us, freely and unconditionally. I pray the contents herein would be a bridge to wherever their journey takes them. In your precious and beautiful name I pray. Amen.

Acknowledgments

My first thank you, of course, is to my Lord, who has given me the burden for others to know him more personally. I thank him for his encouragement, patience, and the working of his Holy Spirit each and every time I turned on my computer. This completed manuscript exists simply because he made it happen and because he gave me the faith to believe that it would.

I thank my loving husband and best friend, Denny, for believing in me and gently nudging me to keep at it when I felt inadequate and when I didn't believe I could write anything worth publishing. He definitely was a rainbow in my cloud.

My family, friends, and even strangers were all encouraging, and I could feel their prayers on days when I needed refreshing. I thank God for every one of them in my life. I am truly blessed and am so excited for them to see the results of this long-awaited product. To God be the glory!

Last but certainly not least, I thank my readers and pray for all those who see the light and feel the peace of a God who has patiently waited for them to know and understand even the smallest portion of his divine grace. Enjoy!

January 1

A Storm Is Never outside the
Hem of Jesus' Robe

God is all-encompassing. I like to picture his cloak embracing me as a cover protects a rosebush through the cold winter. The rosebush painlessly endures the dark, the biting wind, and the frosty nights and is unable to show its beauty for months.

When spring arrives, the bush appears stronger and more beautiful than before. While we are in our storm, Jesus will be our protector and will walk with us hand in hand until the sun shines on our victory.

> You are my hiding place; you will protect me from trouble and surround me with songs of deliverance. (Psalm 32:7)

> People brought all their sick to him and begged him to let the sick just touch the edge of his cloak, and all who touched him were healed. (Matthew 14:36)

January 2

Who Is Packing Your Parachute?

Imagine the final thoughts of the person jumping from the plane or helicopter. I would imagine it would be something like *Well, I hope whoever packed the chute knew what he or she was doing!* The person jumps and hopes to reach the designated spot. Who are you trusting? Through our belief in Jesus, we can trust that God will make our paths straight. When we acknowledge him in all our ways, we know he will cause us to land precisely where he planned. Would you want to be anywhere else?

Trust in the Lord with all your heart and lean not on your own understanding. In all your ways acknowledge him, and he will make your paths straight. (Proverbs 3:5–6)

In God, whose word I praise, in God I trust; I will not be afraid. What can mortal man do to me? (Psalm 56:4)

January 3

Adam and Eve Had a Perfect Parent

Having raised two children, these words really touched my heart. Raising kids is the toughest job in the world. By the time my boys were reaching adolescence and began making decisions on their own, I felt responsible and sometimes guilty for some of their choices. In a Bible study about free will, I rested in the thought that even though God is in control, he gives us free will to make choices. We are not responsible for our children's choices. So don't beat yourself up thinking, *if you had been a better parent maybe they would have been better off.* God was Adam and Eve's parent, and they still made bad choices—to the detriment of us all. The best we can do is pray and ask God to lead our children on solid ground and along his path.

Teach me to do your will for you are my God; may your good spirit lead me on solid ground. (Psalm 143:10)

Children, obey your parents in everything, for this pleases the Lord. (Colossians 3:20)

January 4

Don't Settle for Less than What God Wants to Give

Through the years I have often settled for less because of my feeling of unworthiness or insecurity; other times it was because I was impatient. I've

learned that if I keep his ways and seek his will, he will reward me. When we pray and don't receive what we've asked for, we should expect that God is working out something in our lives that could possibly produce an even greater result. Delay is not denial. So many times things have turned out better than I ever could have imagined. It's all in God's timing. Let things fall into place. It was a thirty-year journey for Jesus to come forth and become the Savior of the world.

> He brought me out into a spacious place; he rescued me because he delighted in me. The Lord has dealt with me according to my righteousness; according to the cleanness of my hands he has rewarded me. (Psalm 18:19–20)

January 5

God Doesn't Comfort Us to Make Us Comfortable
He Comforts Us to Make Us Comforters

We can't give away something we don't have, right? We can't comfort someone unless we have been comforted at some time in our lives. So we can think of giving comfort as a gift. And once it is received, it will then be passed on and will be unending; re-gifting, so to speak. When we suffer, we learn to endure and understand others' sufferings. We can often look back and see how God was there for us, comforting us with his mercy. Compassion is a deep, soulful attribute given to us to be given away.

> Praise be to the God and Father of our Lord Jesus Christ, the Father of compassion and the God of all comfort who comforts us in all our troubles, so that we can comfort those in any trouble with the comfort we ourselves have received from God. (2 Corinthians 1:3–4)

January 6

If Your Seed Is to Come Forth,
It Must Fall to the Ground

If we are to become everything God intends us to be, we must let go of our own desires and seek only his will. Once we do that, with the help of the Holy Spirit, the very thing he wants for us becomes our desire. Plant yourself in God's word and commit yourself wholly to him. Use a flower garden as an example. When we planted our small canna lily bulbs in the spring, by June they would reach eight feet tall—full of abundance and substance. They are a beauty to behold, as they show off their huge crimson-red blooms and purple variegated leaves. It's breathtaking, to say the least. If we believe that's how God sees us, we also will blossom into something to behold—all to the glory of God. Don't settle for less than what God wants to give you.

> But seek first his kingdom and his righteousness, and all these things will be given to you as well. (Matthew 6:33)

> I tell you the truth, unless a kernel of wheat falls to the ground and dies, it remains only a single seed. But if it dies, it produces many seeds. (John 12:24)

January 7

Jesus Himself Taught Us How to Pray

Prayer is simply talking to God—and listening for his response. Prayer is a fragrant language between you and the Lord. It's kind of like a dance. You're in step to the same beat. He leads; you follow. It is total freedom to express yourself before the God who created you. His response may or may not be exactly what you expected, but you can be assured he has your best interest in mind. If you keep his will in mind, you are apt to reap more than you sowed. God is attentive to your prayer. As you pray, listen to his soft voice and know that he is pleased to hear from you. His Sprit is intertwining with yours!

For the eyes of the Lord are on the righteous and his ears are attentive to their prayer. (1 Peter 3:12)

For this is how you should pray. (Matthew 6:9)

January 8

God's Will—the Lord's Prayer

It is extremely interesting to decipher this prayer. It not only acknowledges our Father in heaven but also shows us how we should submit to his will and ask him to fill our needs, pardon our sins, and protect us from the snares of the devil. Praying for God's will to be done requires us to continue to trust in him even when he doesn't answer the way we were hoping. Just before Jesus's death on the cross, Jesus is in the garden praying, and he says to his Father in heaven, "Father, if it is possible, may this cup be taken from me. Yet not as I will but as you will." Jesus gives us so many great examples of prayer. If he goes away into a quiet place to pray, don't you think we should too? I want to be able to pray as he did: "This is what I want, Lord, but if it is not in your plan at this time, I will continue to trust you. No matter what!"

Jesus says, "This then, is how you should pray." (Matthew 6:9)

Going a little farther, he fell with his face to the ground and prayed, "My Father, if it is possible, may this cup be taken from me. Yet not as I will, but as you will." (Matthew 26:39)

January 9

Faith Is Walking in the Dark with God

People are afraid of the dark simply because they don't know what's in it. The dark reveals no beauty, and it is exceedingly empty and mysterious. The silence is sometimes deafening. The only way most people would venture into a dark tunnel is if they could see a light at the other end. And even then they may not find an exit. The security of God's light allows

us to go down any road with trust and confidence. When God lights the darkness, you will never stumble. Look intently for his light. It is an eternal beacon.

> We live by faith; not by sight. (2 Corinthians 5:7)

> Even though I walk through the valley of the shadow of death, I will fear no evil, for you are with me; your rod and your staff, they comfort me. (Psalm 23:4)

January 10

Natural Change Might Preclude a Spiritual Change

Energy produces energy. Change produces change. Most things are a result of themselves. Our move to a different city precluded a spiritual change; there were new surroundings, a new job, new friends, a new church, new trials, new blessings, and new thoughts. We were changed people. Even though it was difficult to leave lifelong friends and a loving family, we felt led to go. Each time we've moved, God has placed us in a spiritual growth pattern. There was a purpose for us in every place. We grew tremendously in our faith and closer to God and met so many Christian people who have now been by our side through thick and thin. Places and friends are gifts from God. Natural change is like a box of chocolates—you never know what you're gonna get! I often think about Abraham and how often God told him to go elsewhere. He actually would have changed history if he hadn't been obedient.

> The Lord had said to Abram, "Leave your country, your people and your father's household and go to the land I will show you. I will make you into a great nation and I will bless you; I will make your name great, and you will be a blessing. I will bless those who bless you, and whoever curses you I will curse; and all peoples on earth will be blessed through you." So, Abram left, as the Lord had told him. (Genesis 12:1–4)

January 11

Shallow Roots Won't Produce a Strong Tree

Have you ever considered how many oak trees are still standing after a huge storm? An oak tree is labeled as a hard wood. It is amazingly strong and durable and grows to astronomical heights, sometimes one hundred feet or more. Not only does it provide wood for homes and furniture and necessary shade, but after the tree matures to about twenty years old, it produces acorns as food for our wildlife as well. The main reason for its strength and durability is its deep roots. It's as if they know they are strong and beautiful as they show off their glory all summer and fall. Just as God is our strength, if we are rooted in him, nothing will tear us down. Like the oak tree in the storm, we will prove to be strong, and when the problems of life seek to pull us down, we will be the last one standing. Let God provide you with the spiritual food and care you need to let his glory shine through. Even though Jesus was born in a rundown stable, I wonder if his cradle was made from a strong oak tree. It just seems right, doesn't it?

For the joy of the Lord is my strength. (Nehemiah 8:10)

The Lord is my strength and my shield. (Psalm 28:7)

He is our corner stone for a sure foundation. (Isaiah 28:16)

January 12

Sometimes We Feel Guilty Not for the Evil We Did But for the Kindness We Didn't Do

Kindness is one of the nine fruits of the Holy Spirit: love, joy, peace, patience, kindness, goodness, faithfulness, gentleness, and self-control (Galatians 5:22–23). We experience God's kindness every day through his grace and forgiveness. It is a gift that needs to be passed on to others. It goes with the adage that it is more blessed to give than to receive. If you have a cordial thought about someone, let him or her know. Give it

away and it will come back to you tenfold. Your act of kindness could lead someone to Christ. All that is necessary for evil to triumph is for good people to stand by and do nothing.

> Make sure that nobody pays back wrong for wrong, but always try to be kind to each other and to everyone else. (1 Thessalonians 5:15)

> Love is patient, love is kind. (1 Corinthians 13:4)

January 13

Your Children Are Your Message to a World You Will Never See

Remember, children learn what they live. They will pass on to their children and grandchildren all the things they learned from you, some good, some not so good. We are God's messengers and are commissioned to spread the good news about Jesus. Bringing our children up to know the Lord intimately will bring God's message to future generations. You and your children and their children will be blessed for your obedience. It's a proven fact that children who have God in their life experience less depression and trouble, more love, and feel better about themselves. They will most likely end up living in a world where you no longer exist. Give them a part of yourself, and they will pass it on.

> How, then, can they call on the one they have not believed in? And how can they believe in the one of whom they have not heard? And how can they hear without someone preaching to them? And how can they preach unless they are sent? As it is written, "how beautiful are the feet of those who bring good news!" (Romans 10:14–15)

January 14

To be Left Unmolested by Satan
Is No Evidence of Blessing

Do you ever get the impression that some people think they are blessed because they don't have any trials or aren't going through any hard times? I've learned through experience that the closer I get to God and the more I turn my life over to him through Jesus Christ, the more Satan throws obstacles in my way. It only makes sense if you are sitting on the fence and are unsure if you want to be in God's world or Satan's, Satan probably won't waste much time on you. However, if you have gotten off the fence and have both feet planted firmly in God's world, Satan doesn't like that because he wants to keep you from growing in your faith. He doesn't like to lose that battle with God. We need trials to build character and strength for growth to get us where God can use us in his plan. That's where the blessing comes in!

> Consider it pure joy, my brothers, whenever you face trials of many kinds, because you know that the testing of your faith develops perseverance. Perseverance must finish its work so that you may be mature and complete, not lacking anything. (James 1:2–4)

January 15

Living for an Audience of One

If you look closely, you can see God in the bleachers cheering you on. He's not particularly for either side, but he is there for you. He knows how many goals you'll make and how many times you'll fumble. He knows every play you will need to execute, and that there was never a practice called. No matter the weather, he'll never miss a game. He'll be an encourager at halftime and will never leave early. He's there for you, and at the end of the game, he will say, "Well done, my good and faithful servant." (Matthew 25:21)

So we fix our eyes not on what is seen, but on what is unseen. (2 Corinthians 4:18)

January 16

Quarreling with the Process of God

Have you ever tried assisting God in a particular situation; manipulating circumstances to better the outcome? Just a little bit? I've done it myself and have watched others do it for years. It's never worked well for me. How about you? I know each time I tried, the Holy Spirit showed me something in myself that needed to be wiped clean. God has done a great deal of scrubbing in my life, and I'm quite sure he hasn't put his scrub brush away. The cleansing always brings about freshness and a new level of obedience to him. Take Job, for example, and learn from his perseverance and faith. We all need to remember that the same God who came to earth to die for our sins is the same God who is the author of our lives. Always wait for him to act on your behalf, and you will never pick your mercies green.

In all this, Job did not sin by charging God with wrong doing. (Job 1:22)

He who has clean hands and a pure heart, who does not lift up his soul to an idol or swear by what is false. He will receive blessing from the Lord and vindication from God his Savior. (Psalm 24:4–5)

January 17

Jesus Never Promised an Easy Passage but a Safe Landing

Trust and obey. He has always been a shelter from the storm. Call on his name in time of trouble. Exalt his holy name, and he will lift you up. When Jesus left the earth, God sent us the Holy Spirit to guide and comfort us. Use him as your compass, and you will always find his way. Many winding roads are ahead of you; some will have street signs, some

won't. When you come to a fork in the road, which way will you go? Let God be your guide. He has an aerial view and knows your way home. Trust … and obey.

> I sought the Lord and he answered me; he delivered me from all my fears. (Psalm 34:4)

> The name of the Lord is a strong tower; the righteous run to it and are safe. (Proverbs 18:10)

January 18

Consider the Value of Affliction

This scripture below from 2 Corinthians is about Paul going through physical pain. Paul became weak and felt he was not able to handle the situation. He asked God three times to remove the burden. God reminds Paul that God's power is made perfect in our weakness and tells him that God's grace is sufficient for him. God was actually allowing Paul to go through that trial as a means of keeping him humble. God knew exactly what he was doing. It's a great story and one that reminds us that we are not alone in our sorrows. Even though it may seem God is nowhere to be found, he is there and is working in you and for you. Keep going. You may not see the results until you walk farther down the road.

> Blessed is the man whom God corrects; so do not despise the discipline of the Almighty. For He wounds, but he also binds up; he injures, but his hands also heal. (Job 5:17–18)

> Three times I pleaded with the Lord to take it away from me. But he said to me, "My grace is sufficient for you, for my power is made perfect in weakness." (2 Corinthians 12:8–9)

January 19

Accepting Jesus Must be through the Heart—Not the Intellect

In the book of John, Jesus, conversing with the Jews, says, "You diligently study the Scriptures because you think that by them you possess eternal life. These are the scriptures that testify about me, yet you refuse to come to me to have life" (5:39–40). This is a great example of intellect verses the heart. They didn't get it! Here was their Messiah right in front of them and they were blind to the truth. Jesus wanted to set them free, but their hearts were hardened to the truth he spoke. You can talk about the scriptures, even memorize the entire Bible, but if you can't move the truth from your brain to your heart, you have not yet received the gift. Know the truth, and the truth will set you free. You need to "live it" not just "think it."

> The Lord looks at the heart. (1 Samuel 16:7)

January 20

If You Don't Know Where You're Going, You'll Never Know When You've Arrived

You don't need to go through this life blindly. God has the correct map to every place he has destined you to go. Let him be the navigator. He doesn't promise that the road will always be smooth, but he does promise he will be there as you go over every bump and hit every pothole. There will be signs to read along the way, and if you have your spiritual spectacles on, you will be able to read them clearly. Did you ever wish you could have an aerial view of where you were headed? If you use Jesus as your guide, you will hear him say, "This is the way, walk in it" (Isaiah 30:21). Ask him to keep you on that straight and narrow path that leads straight to his door. He's waiting and will leave the light on for you.

> In spite of this, you did not trust in the Lord your God, who went ahead of you on your journey, in fire by night and in a cloud by day, to search out places for you to camp and to show you the way you should go. (Deuteronomy 1:32–33)

January 21

Don't Allow the Past to Influence the Future

All you have is today. The past is gone, and tomorrow may never come. Of course you can always reminisce about the good old days, about events or people who bring a smile to your face. I believe the scripture below from Isaiah points to times in our lives that bring us pain or guilt or fear—memories we can't build on and use as a foundation for tomorrow. Instead of letting the past get you down, use each of those negatives as a rung on a ladder and climb to where God wants you to be today. He can always bring good out of a bad situation. Look for it. The higher you get, the further you'll see.

Forget the former things; do not dwell on the past. (Isaiah 43:18)

January 22

Jesus said, "Except you die you shall not live."

You can look at the word *live* as in a physical sense; not really giving much thought to life until you know it is about to end, or you could give some thought to the spiritual side of life. Jesus said, "Except you die you shall not live." It may be difficult at first to understand the phrase *die to self*. All it really refers to is you taking yourself out of the equation of your life. Jesus + Nothing = Salvation. It's not about you. It's all about him having the right place in your life.

In him we live and move and have our being. (Acts 17:28)

For to me, to live is Christ and to die is gain. (Philippians 1:21)

January 23

Don't Grow Weary of Doing Good

The below scripture from Galatians can cover a multitude of areas in our lives. Perseverance can run very thin if we don't have the hope or faith to keep going. Even our Lord Jesus Christ called out to his Father during his last hours. He was exhausted and weary as he asked God to take away the cup he was about to drink, and God said no. Remember, it is God's will we should be praying for, not ours. The last key may be the one that unlocks the door. Don't stop short of a miracle! Jesus took the necessary steps to the cross in order to save us from our sins. Look to Jesus as an example when you feel like giving up.

> Let us not become weary in doing good, for at the proper time we will reap a harvest if we do not give up. (Galatians 6:9)

> But do not forget this one thing, dear friends: With the Lord a day is like a thousand years, and a thousand years are like a day. The Lord is not slow in keeping his promise, as some understand slowness. He is patient with you, not wanting anyone to perish, but everyone to come to repentance. (2 Peter 3:8–9)

January 24

Don't Put Your Hope in Wealth

We've all experienced someone who depended on their income and success to make them happy and financially secure. In our jobs, if we depend on man or ourselves to make us successful, we are walking on pretty shaky ground. There is no such thing as financial security as most of us can testify. Realizing that God is in control of every aspect of our lives, including our finances, is the first step. Put your hope in God and you will be blessed. Let go of filling your void with material things or high status. When you give it all over to him, he will eventually cause all of his desires to be yours. The tighter you hold onto your money, the less value it actually has. If you don't have God, you have nothing. And what does it profit a man to gain the whole world but lose his own soul? (Mark 8:36)

Not to put their hope in wealth, which is so uncertain, but to put their hope in God. (1 Timothy 6:17–18)

Whatever you do, work at it with all your heart, as working for the Lord, not for men. (Colossians 3:23)

January 25

Adversity Introduces Us to Ourselves

When you experience something of great magnitude, such as the 9-11 terrorist attack or the Boston Marathon bombing, you are reminded that you are not in control. Psalm 46:10 has helped me through many adverse situations and has become my favorite. It's very difficult to be still and realize that God doesn't need our help. Although they cut deep into our souls, those assaults were no surprise to him. Many times he wants to wake us up and make us realize what is important in this world. He wants us to look at our families, our country, and ourselves, and he desires our attention. Adversity is not in his vocabulary, but he uses it to help us find him. We are nothing without God. Look to him. Give him the right place in your life.

Be still and know that I am God. (Psalm 46:10)

If my people, who are called by my name, will humble themselves and pray and seek my face and turn from their wicked ways, then will I hear from heaven and will forgive their sin and will heal their land. (2 Chronicles 7:14)

January 26

God Doesn't Call the Able;
He Uses the Available

Moses was called by the Lord to deliver Israel. God spoke to him from the burning bush (Exodus 3:1–5) and told him he was going to send him to

Pharaoh to bring the Israelites out of Egypt (v. 11). Moses, afraid, didn't think he was qualified and said, "Who am I, that I should go to Pharaoh and bring the Israelites out of Egypt?" And God said, "I will be with you" (vv. 11–12). God never gives us a difficult situation without giving us the grace to get through it. Many of the people God called for his service in the Old and New Testament were unqualified for the job, but through faith and perseverance, they got the job done. Don't be afraid to step out on the water as Peter did. Keep your focus on Jesus, not on yourself. When you think you might hear God calling your name, just say, "I'm here, Lord. What is it you want me to do?"

> Moses said to the Lord, "Oh Lord, I have never been eloquent, neither in the past or since you have spoken to your servant. I am slow of speech and tongue." The Lord said to him, "Who gave man his mouth? Who makes him deaf or mute? Who gives him sight or makes him blind? Is it not I, the Lord? Now go; I will help you speak and teach you what to say." (Exodus 4:10–12)

January 27

Good Works Are the Result of Salvation, Not the Cause

So many people are so busy "doing" that they forget to "be." God blesses your endeavors to "do" things for him, but what he truly desires is for you to "be" with him—having a closer relationship with him, seeking his face. Don't let your business at church be considered your time with the Lord. He wants you—alone, all to himself, on your knees in a quiet place. That's why you were created—to give him pleasure. If we could get to heaven by doing good, just how good would we need to be? That leaves it too open-ended, doesn't it? Think about it. If you could get to heaven by being good, Jesus died for nothing.

> For it is by Grace you have been saved, through faith—and this is not from yourselves, it is the gift of God—not by works so that no one can boast. (Ephesians 2:8–9)

> It's not by works. (Romans 11:6)

January 28

Refuse to be Overcome

Depending on your age, you have probably persevered little or persevered much. Whatever the case, hopefully you have given the credit and the glory to the Holy Spirit. His gentle and consistent leading has brought you through to the other side where things look different and are explained. You hold onto your faith and refuse to be overcome because you know that God stands by his promises. The Father, Son, and Holy Spirit all stand behind those promises. It's like a tug-of-war with all of them on your side of the imaginary line.

> To him who overcomes, I will give the right to eat from the tree of life, which is in the paradise of God. (Revelation 2:7)

> You need to persevere so that when you have done the will of God, you will receive what he has promised. (Hebrews 10:36)

> Blessed is the man who perseveres under trial, because when he has stood the test, he will receive the crown of life that God has promised to those who love him. (James 1:12)

> Do not be overcome with evil, but overcome evil with good. (Romans 12:21)

January 29

You Must Be Born Again

"Born again" is simply a change of the heart; it's wanting God more than we want sin.

In John 3:3, Jesus is speaking to Nicodemus, a member of the Jewish ruling council, who was spiritually blinded by the Jewish law. God had spoken to Nicodemus about having eternal life through Jesus (John 3:16), so he secretly sought out Jesus to ask him further about this. Even though

Nicodemus was a religious teacher, he knew nothing about the spiritual birth and felt a void in his life. He did not understand how you could be born again spiritually. In the verses that follow, Jesus teaches Nicodemus what it all meant, and he believed Jesus by faith. We are born naturally and then "born again" spiritually when we accept the things of God, including salvation through no one but Jesus. You, too, must turn your eyes upon Jesus and by faith look straight into his glorious face and believe. You will never be the same again.

> Jesus declared, "I tell the truth, no one can see the kingdom of God unless he is born again." (John 3:3)

January 30

Tithing:
He Doesn't Look at What We Give
He Looks at What We Keep

In Malachi 3, God talks about robbing him through tithes and offerings. Verse 10 says, "Bring the whole tithe into the storehouse, that there may be food in my house. Test me in this, says the Lord Almighty, and see if I will not throw open the floodgates of heaven and pour out so much blessing that you will not have room enough for it." Who would pass up that promise from the Lord? The Bible says there is a great distinction between those who serve God and those who do not. Consider it a privilege to give to the Lord and, like fasting, don't let anyone know about your giving so you will receive blessings from the Lord for your obedience and not praise from man. Which would you rather have? Spiritual blessings or worldly praise? What has the world ever given but turmoil and sorrow? The only one we can put total trust in is God. He has promised he will always be there for us. He will not break his promises. They are written with His blood.

> A tithe of everything from the land, whether grain from the soil or fruit from the trees belongs to the Lord; it is holy to the Lord. (Leviticus 27:30)

January 31

Sin: Direct Opposition to God's Will

That's pretty straightforward, isn't it? But how do you know the will of God? You can always ask him! He will tell you because it's his will that you know. That's why he gave you the Bible, the blueprint for your life. You could look at the Ten Commandments in Deuteronomy 5 or read what Jesus had to say on the Sermon on the Mount about the beatitudes in Matthew 5. If you are not living in Christ's will, you will know it. The Holy Spirit will gently nudge you and make you aware of any wickedness in you. Then you are to act on it.

> Search me, O God and know my heart; test me and know my anxious thoughts. See if there is any offensive way in me and lead me in the way everlasting. (Psalm 139:24)

February 1

Fortune-Telling Involves an Evil Spirit

The Bible pinpoints fortune-telling as evil. It would be a temptation to know the future rather than trusting your heavenly Father is in control and has a plan for you. If you lived your life according to what a fortune-teller reveals, it would change every blessing God might be planning on your behalf. Some of the things you do may end up seemingly good and right, but they could never compare to God's plan. Just the excitement of waking up each new morning with great expectation of what God is going to do in your life far outweighs thinking you know the day before. Hmm … probably best to weigh that one out, right?

> Once when we were going to the place of prayer, we were met by a slave girl who had a spirit by which she predicted the future. She earned a great deal of money for her owners by fortune-telling. This girl followed Paul and the rest of us, shouting, "These men are servants of the Most High God who are telling you the way to be saved." She kept this up for many days. Finally Paul became so troubled the he turned around and said to the spirit, "In the

name of Jesus Christ I command you to come out of her!" At that moment the spirit left her. (Acts 16:16–18)

February 2

Consider Your Sorrow as Payment for a Harp String

Sorrow: a deep distress, sadness, or regret. So are they saying much sadness would create a melody, a sweet or agreeable sound?

A harp with only one string could never tell a story. In order to convey a picture with words, you would need all the necessary strings, usually anywhere from twelve to ninety.

Harps are generally found at celebrations. In the Old Testament, it was often the instrument used to praise the Lord and offer sacrifices. Over my lifetime, I have praised God mostly after he has brought victory after sorrow. I've learned to use my harp strings to praise God for my trials. Praise brings us into a pinnacle of fellowship and intimacy with our God.

> And yet I will praise him! (Job 13:15)

> Blessed are those who have learned to acclaim you, who walk in the light of your presence, O Lord. (Psalm 89:15)

February 3

God Has Nothing Worthwhile Having That Is Easily Attained

Accomplishing an easy task just doesn't bring the same satisfaction as accomplishing something you never dreamed you could do. The easiest way is not always the best way. Although, that is what most of us choose. Besides salvation, I see the most worthwhile gift God has given me is the fruit of the Holy Spirit: love, joy, peace, patience, kindness, goodness,

gentleness, faithfulness, and self-control (Galatians 5:22). In order to receive this fruit, we must first get past the "obedience" barrier. That would be our part because it involves our free will. Is that easy for you? I struggle with it every day. I'm sure I have lost many blessings because of it. But I know when I am focused on Jesus I am filled to the rim with the fruit of the Holy Spirit. I am drinking from my saucer because my cup is overflowing! Remember, if you go around the mountain to get to the other side, you will miss the view from the top.

If you love me you will keep my commandments. (John 15:14)

February 4

Nonbelievers Will Be Cut Off

The scriptures below say that only those who believe in God's Son, Jesus, will have eternal life in heaven. They say that for those who do not believe there will be weeping and gnashing of teeth. These words are written in red, which portray Jesus' very words. Jesus didn't say, "If you are a good person, I will let you in." Being a good person is a characteristic of a saved person but not how a person gets saved. I guess I would rather believe and be wrong than to not believe and face eternal damnation and never see the face of Jesus. Which will you choose?

Whoever believes in the Son has eternal life, but whoever rejects the Son will not see life, for God's wrath remains on him. (John 3:36)

The Son of Man will send out his angels, and they will weed out of his kingdom everything that causes sin and all who do evil. They will throw them into the fiery furnace, where there will be weeping and gnashing of teeth. (Matthew 13:41–42)

February 5

Sitting Still and Waiting on God Involves Tremendous Strength

If you choose to make something happen rather than wait for God's leading, you could very well miss a greater blessing. That is called "picking your mercies green." Many times I have chosen to pluck my fruit from the tree before it has ripened. Oh yes, I could still eat it, but it wasn't as sweet as it would have been. The strength to wait comes from the Holy Spirit. He will tell you the exact moment of fully ripened fruit. And when he reveals this to you, move on it. Pick the fruit, and see how easy it comes off the vine. Oh, how sweet it is!

> Be still and know that I am God. (Psalm 46:10)

> Yet the Lord longs to be gracious to you; he rises to show you compassion. For the Lord is a God of justice. Blessed are all who wait for him! (Isaiah 30:18)

February 6

When We Are Born Again, Our Spirit Comes Alive to God

It is a fresh beginning, a lifelong process of becoming Christ-like. It is like going from death to life, from darkness to light, from decayed to fresh. Being born again is a spiritual rebirth. It happens to you when you realize there is something bigger than yourself—something of substance—a far greater truth. You will know it when it happens. It will be a "wow" moment. And life will never be the same—this life and the afterlife.

> In reply Jesus declared, "I tell you the truth, no one can see the kingdom of God unless he is born again." (John 3:3)

> He who began a good work in you will carry it on to completion until the day of Christ Jesus. (Philippians 1:6)

February 7

Friends Are a Gift from God

My VBF is Jesus Christ, and yes, sometimes I wish I could text him. Seriously though, he has supplied me with many other BFFs. I have close relationships with friends I met over forty years ago. Some are silver; some are gold. Some are born again; some are seeking the truth. Any one of them would be at my beck and call. I pray for them and their families. It's a bond only God can hold together. I'm not saying that we've never had disagreements or that we all come out of the same mold. But our love for one another stems from one main cord: Jesus Christ. We consider each other as gifts from him. In Ecclesiastes 4:12, it says a cord of three strands is not quickly broken: you, God, and me.

> I thank my God every time I remember you. In all my prayers for you, I always pray with joy. (Philippians 1:3–4)

February 8

You Are Chosen by the Father as a Gift to His Son

Imagine God giving a gift to Jesus. Now imagine that the gift is you. He plucked you out of your dirty, sinful life, cleaned you up, wrapped you in beautifully embossed paper, and said, "Here, this is my most magnificent gift to you." Then Jesus reveals God to you through himself and gives you back to God! Through this selfless giving, you have been made one with God and are loved by him with the same love he gives to Jesus. It doesn't get much better than that! Maybe you should read that again!

> I have revealed you to those whom you gave me out of the world. They were yours, you gave them to me. (John 17:6)

> I pray for them. I am not praying for the world, but for those you have given me, for they are yours. (John 17:9)

February 9

Things Happen to Give God Glory

The following scripture tells the story about a man who was blind from birth.

"Jesus' disciples asked Jesus, 'Who sinned, this man or his parents that he was born blind?' Jesus answers, 'Neither this man or his parents sinned, but this happened so that the work of God might be displayed in his life'" (John 9:1–3). When we are sensitive to the ways of God, we can be blessed by someone's so-called disabilities. We need to know that God doesn't cause these things but rather allows particular burdens so he will be glorified in his people so others might be saved. God works in mysterious ways.

> And call upon me in the day of trouble; I will deliver you, and you will honor me. (Psalm 50:15)

February 10

Ask God to Show You Your Sin

If you like your life the way it is, don't ask God to show you your sin because he will definitely upset the apple cart. In fact, he will make applesauce out of you! God will always find something that needs work because we are a work in progress. When he shows you an area in your life that needs improving, don't argue with him. Let him gently nudge you through the work of the Holy Spirit. When he removes something that he doesn't approve of, he will replace it with something you never even knew you wanted. His desire becomes your desire. Your desire to serve him becomes greater than your desire not to.

> Search me Oh God and see if there be any wicked way in me. (Psalm 139:23–24)

> He who conceals his sins does not prosper, but whoever confesses and renounces them finds mercy. (Proverbs 28:13)

February 11

Consulting Witches and Mediums Moves You into a Whole New Realm

Have you ever seen a medium or one who hears from the dead? I've always been curious to know how they pull off fooling so many people. Is it a trick of the devil? Or do they have just enough persuasion to attract people? Are people that gullible to think someone has the power to hear from dead people? As the scripture says, "Should not a people inquire of their God?" (Isaiah 8:19). Do you have a loved one who died before you could forgive him or her or before you were forgiven? Maybe before some problem was not resolved? Seek God's grace and tender mercies to heal your memory or your burden. If you are his child, he will do that for you. Put your hope in the living God (1 Timothy 4:10).

> When men tell you to consult mediums and spirits who whisper and mutter, should not a people inquire of their God? Why consult the dead on behalf of the living. (Isaiah 8:19)

> Let no one be found among you who sacrifices his son or daughter in the fire, who practices divination or sorcery, interprets omens, engages in witchcraft, or casts spells, or who is a medium or spiritist or who consults the dead. (Deuteronomy 18:10–11)

February 12

Following Evil Spirits in the End Times

Only those who are in a close personal relationship with Christ will be able to survive the days to come. They are the only people who will even recognize the end times. It would be like never being taught about abuse; you wouldn't recognize it if you weren't looking for the signs. Many books in the New Testament refer to the end of the world as we know it. The book of Revelation lays it all out, the events leading up to it and what to expect until Christ's return. I would encourage you to seek out a Bible study of the book of Revelation. And note that the word *revelation* is singular. It is one revelation given to John by God, and is so interesting

and totally awesome. Study it! This book is very difficult to read on your own because it is full of symbolism. You need someone who has studied the book in depth to help you understand it. It is actually beautiful. When you read and understand it, the end times become sacred instead of scary.

> The Spirit clearly says that in the end times some will abandon the faith and follow deceiving spirits and things taught by demons. (1Timothy 4:1)

February 13

A Proper Time for Everything

Isn't it difficult to know when to act on a decision? Whether trivial or serious, it can sometimes be mind-boggling and even life-changing. The effects of our decisions can hurt us and even extend to others. The very best outcomes happen after we have prayed and asked God to help us. Which church should I join? Who should I vote for? What job would be best for me? Should I allow my child to date this person? Timing is everything. Remember, don't pick your mercies green. Wait until they're ripe!

> Whoever obeys his command will come to no harm and the wise heart will know the proper time and procedure. (Ecclesiastes 8:5)

> There is a time for everything, and a season for every activity under heaven:
> a time to be born, and a time die,
> a time to plant and a time to uproot,
> a time to kill and a time to heal,
> a time to tear down and a time to build,
> a time to weep and a time to laugh,
> a time to mourn and a time to dance,
> a time to scatter stones and a time to gather them,
> a time to embrace and a time to refrain,
> a time to search and a time to give up,
> a time to keep and a time to throw away,
> a time to tear and a time to mend,

a time to be silent and a time to speak,
a time to love and a time to hate,
a time for war and a time for peace. (Ecclesiastes 3:1–8)

February 14

Approaching the Throne in
Our Time of Need

Approaching God's throne can lead you to an opened door. Not seeking his wisdom can lead you to a window you can't reach. I know you've probably heard the saying, "When God closes a door he always opens a window." Have you ever had a door seem to slam in your face and not a window in sight? It could be that you're not on the right street. Someone may have given you the wrong address. Keep seeking God in prayer, receive counsel from godly people, and look for confirmation. God's timing is never off.

> Let us then approach the throne of grace with confidence, so that we may receive mercy and find grace to help us in our time of need. (Hebrews 4:16)

February 15

Jesus was with the Father
before the World Began

The Holy Trinity: Father God, Son Jesus, and the Holy Spirit. Only by faith can we assume to understand this. In the book of John, Jesus thanks God for his (Jesus') former glory of being in God's presence. In John 1:1, you can actually replace "the word" with "Jesus." They are synonyms. John 1:14 states, "The word became flesh and dwelt among us." That's Jesus! Read John 1:1 again: "In the beginning was the Word, and the Word was with God and the Word was God. He was with God in the beginning." God inspired scripture. This is truth. Believe and walk in it.

And now, Father, glorify me in your presence with the glory I had with you before the world began. (John 17:5)

February 16

Religion: Man's Efforts to Get to God
Christianity: God's Efforts to Get to Man

Being born again is what changes religion into a relationship. In the Merriam-Webster dictionary, "relationship" is defined as the state of being related. "Related" means connected through membership in the same family. "Religion" is defined as the service and worship of God or the supernatural; a personal system of religious beliefs or attitudes. Relationship is about a Who (a person) while religion is about a what (a thing). Some people sing *about* God (religious) and others sing *to* God (relationship). The only way we can have that personal relationship with God is by accepting his gift of Jesus. It's called "being born again." First we are born physically through our mother and then born again spiritually through Jesus. Jesus said, "I am the way, the truth and the life; no one comes to the Father except through me." (John 14:6)

> I tell you the truth, no one can see the Kingdom of God unless he is born again. (John 3:4)

February 17

God Will Send Rain in Due Season

When our bills arrive, they usually have a due date for payment. Sometimes the invoice states there is an amount that is past due. Did we forget or not understand what they wanted? Did we have too many things going on to remember? Were we too busy? Or did we just not care about our commitment to the other party? Aren't you relieved that we don't have to send God a past-due notice? Isn't it good that he is faithful about the commitment he has made to us? He knows our needs. He is never late, and he doesn't need any reminders. He knows when we are dry and when

to send the rain. It comes when we are ready to receive it. It's a reward for obedience. Wait for it. It will be so refreshing!

> If you follow my decrees and are careful to obey my commands, I will send you rain in its season and the ground will yield crops and the trees of the field their fruit. (Leviticus 26:3–4)

> I will look on you with favor and make you fruitful and increase your numbers, and I will keep my covenant with you. (Leviticus 26:9)

February 18

God Doesn't Bless Us for What We Know But for Our Responses to What We Know

We can join Bible studies, listen to the sermons, read books, and meet in Christian groups, but if we don't share our knowledge with others, where is the blessing? Peter knew who Christ was, but when it came down to admitting it and standing up for Jesus, he failed miserably. His response was exactly as Jesus had said, that he would deny knowing Jesus. Peter's fear and pride got in the way. There was too much "self" left in him. That is the lesson taught here. If we want others to see Jesus in us, we must have Christ-like responses, and that can only happen when we allow God to change us. He removes something in us to make room for himself.

> I tell you, Peter, before the rooster crows today, you will deny three times that you know me. (Luke 22:34)

> A servant girl saw him seated there in the firelight. She looked closely at him and said, "This man was with him." But he denied it. "Woman, I don't know him," he said. A little later someone else saw him and said, "You also are one of them." "Man, I am not!" Peter replied. About an hour later another asserted, "Certainly this fellow was with him, for he is a Galilean." Peter replied, "Man, I don't know what you're talking about!" Just as he was speaking the rooster crowed. The Lord turned and looked straight at Peter. Then Peter remembered the word the Lord had

spoken to him: "Before the rooster crows today, you will disown me three times." And he went outside and wept bitterly. (Luke 22:56–62)

February 19

"A Cord of Three Strands Is Not Quickly Broken"
(Ecclesiastes 4:12)

This verse relates to unity, standing firm in one spirit. I see the two strands as two people and the third strand as Christ. The uniting of the Holy Spirit in our relationships strengthens them. He helps us to stand firm in our convictions, commitments, and decisions. I love the word harmony. One of Webster's definitions for harmony is "internal calm." Who can calm you internally? No one but the Holy Spirit. My husband and I experience that calmness only when we are drenched in the mercies and grace of our Lord. Without him we are nothing.

> Two are better than one, because they have a good return for their work. If one falls down, his friend can help him up. But pity the man who falls and has no one to help him up. Also, if two lie down together, they will keep warm. But how can one keep warm alone? Though one may be overpowered, two can defend themselves. A cord of three strands is not quickly broken. (Ecclesiastes 4:9–12)

I like to think of this chorus from the song, Bind us Together, written by Bob Gillman.

> Bind us together Lord,
> Bind us together
> With cords that cannot be broken.
>
> Bind us together Lord,
> Bind us together
> Bind us together with Love.

February 20

The Stars Belong to God, Not Astrologers

God created the heavens and the earth. It was on the fourth day of creation that he created the stars. On the very same day, he made the sun and the moon. Genesis 1:17 says, "God set them in the expanse of the sky to give light on the earth, to govern the day and the night, and to separate light from darkness. And God saw that it was good." The stars are a gift to us. They were not given to astrologers to foretell the future. Only Jesus knows what is to come. He knew it before we were ever born. Jeremiah 1:5 says, "Before I formed you in the womb, I knew you." Only go to God for your answers. He created the heavens, then the earth, and then *you*!

> In the beginning, God created the heavens and the earth. (Genesis 1:1)

February 21

God Is the Referee: He Rings the Bell

God is our umpire in the game of life, so to speak. Except it's not a game or a rehearsal. We only go around once. Hebrews 9:27 says, "Man is destined to die once and after that to face judgment." God will decide whether we win or lose, whether we hit or miss the mark. It really isn't about what we did but about who we were. Were we his? Did we die to ourselves and give our heart to him? Being born again is a spiritual rebirth and a win-win situation. We are judged the winner and we will get the prize!

> For whoever finds me finds life and receives favor from the Lord. (Proverbs 8:35)

February 22

Whatever You Prepare for
Is What You Will Get

Are you preparing for eternity? Are you excited about your eternal inheritance? The Bible has several verses relating to the prize we have waiting for us. As you know, an inheritance is something set aside for you when someone close to you passes away. The details are written down and put in a safe place in assurance that the beneficiary will receive it. When Jesus died, the details were written in his own blood that you are to receive, with no strings attached, eternal life. You are the beneficiary. No one can take it away. Open your hands and heart and receive it. It's a free gift! It covers you forever!

> For this reason Christ is the mediator of a new covenant, that those who are called may receive the promised eternal inheritance— now that he has died as a ransom to set them free from the sins committed under the first covenant. (Hebrews 9:15)

> And into an inheritance that can never perish, spoil or fade; kept in heaven for you. (1Peter 1:4)

February 23

Faith doesn't change Circumstances;
it only changes You

This hit me like a ton of bricks, producing a bruise that took a long time to heal. It's kind of amazing how long it takes us to figure things out. And then when we do, it all seems so simple. Having faith doesn't change what's in front of you, only what is inside. I can see how I handle things differently from a year ago. My obedience has made me wiser in the Lord. I don't choose to argue with him. I ask and then I say, "Your will be done." It's a hard lesson but a good one. It's called growth.

> We live by faith, not by sight. (2 Corinthians 5:7)

February 24

The Prodigal Son

This is a story of hope. Whether it's about a lost sheep or a wayward child, a parent or a friend, it's about showing mercy. Most times, mercy is undeserved. That's what makes it so great. It's unexpected. It's a gift of love. Sometimes it's even hard to accept. Forgiveness with no questions asked and no strings attached. I gave my dad that gift before he died. I told him I forgave him for not giving me the love I so desperately needed. I told him it was okay. He had lost his father at a young age, and I knew he was never taught how to share his love with his children. You can't give away something you don't have, right? When I set him free, I set myself free as well. It was a God thing. Who do you need to set free? Read the story in Luke about the mercy a father bestowed on his son. Do you see any resemblance to a story in your life? Even if you are finding it difficult to forgive, God can make it possible. And if you need forgiveness, have faith, pray, and wait. The same God who created the universe forgave you. Surely, he can work things out.

(Read Luke Chapter 15 vs 11-32)

February 25

God Feeds by His Hand

No one would choose to starve, would they? I've heard about people fasting for a purpose for a particular amount of time. I've also heard about people who don't believe they need spiritual food. But that would only be those who have never tasted the goodness of God. How sad to not hunger for the things of God—his fellowship, guidance, peace, and love—and the fruit of the Holy Spirit—love, joy, peace, patience, kindness, goodness, gentleness, faithfulness, and self-control. Who doesn't need them? Who? The ones who think they don't are the very ones who need them the most.

> Then Jesus declared, "I am the bread of life. He who comes to me will never go hungry, and he who believes in me will never be thirsty." (John 6:35)

But give me only my daily bread. (Proverbs 30:8)

February 26

Those Who Trust in the One True God, Know Him Intimately

There are so many different religions throughout the world: Hinduism, Buddhism, Islam, Catholic, Protestant, Evangelical, Jehovah Witness, and a host of others I can't begin to pronounce or claim to have any knowledge of. Spiritually born-again Christians are the only people of faith who have a personal relationship with their God. It's a faith whereby we receive something of great significance through no work of our own: a personal relationship with God through his Son, Jesus. All we have to do is ask, and our sins are forgiven, we are set free, and we will spend eternity in heaven. It's free for the asking even though we didn't do anything to deserve it. Jesus said, "Ask, and you will receive, seek and you will find" (Matthew 7:8). It is complexity made simple.

> There is a way that seems right to a man, but in the end it leads to death. (Proverbs 14:12)

> Fear of man will prove to be a snare, but whoever trusts in the Lord is kept safe. (Proverbs 29:25)

February 27

God Never Leaves His Throne

Have you ever felt a tug at your heart or some kind of physical pressure that doesn't make sense to you? You may feel like you need to do something for someone or a pressure to listen. God works from afar. When you feel that nudge, he is working within you through his Holy Spirit. He is saying, "Be still and know I am God" (Psalm 46:10). Although he never leaves his throne, you can feel his presence. He's letting you know that he is there for you, right in the center of your little insignificant universe. If you stay very still, you might hear the rustle of his garment as he goes by.

Be still before the Lord, all mankind, because he has roused himself from his holy dwelling. (Zechariah 2:13)

God reigns over the nations; God is seated on his holy throne. (Psalm 47:8)

February 28

Will God Hold Us Accountable for the Blood of the Wicked?

When I say to a wicked man, "You will surely die," and you do not warn him or speak out to dissuade him from his evil ways in order to save his life; that wicked man will die for his sin, and I will hold you accountable for his blood. But if you do warn the wicked man and he does not turn from his wickedness or from his evil ways, he will die for his sin; but you will have saved yourself. (Ezekiel 3:18–19)

Did you read that twice? I had to, and then I had to mull it over in my mind for a while. This verse is from the Old Testament, and since Jesus made a new covenant with us in the New Testament, this does not hold true for us. We are not responsible for someone else's sin. However, many stories come back to me about others' gratitude for someone sharing the good news about Jesus with them. If someone was starving or freezing and you had food or heat in your back pocket, wouldn't you offer it to him or her? Offering it is our job. It's what God expects of us. Jesus is God's gift to us, and he wants us to pass it on. If you're not passing it on, ask yourself why. It may be your pockets aren't deep enough.

February 29

God Gives Us Power over the Enemy

Did you know we have total authority over the devil and his schemes? We, meaning those of us who have accepted the gift of Jesus. That power became available to us the moment Jesus died on the cross. It's there and ready to use. Speak directly to the devil. Tell him he has no power over

you because you are a child of the King. Sing praises out loud to God and the devil will flee. He can't stand to hear praises going to the one he completely opposes. He knows he has already lost the battle. All you have to do is remind him.

> I have given you authority to trample on snakes and scorpions and to overcome all the power of the enemy; nothing will harm you. (Luke 10:19)

> Submit yourselves then to God. Resist the devil, and he will flee from you. (James 4:7)

March 1

We Could Not Exist without the Moon, Sun, Air, Stars, and Sea

"And God saw that it was good" (Genesis 1:1). That passage is repeated several times in the first chapter of Genesis. God created these phenomenal gifts for us even before he created man. He provided for us before we ever existed! A provision of such magnitude could only come from someone who loved to that degree. He continues to minister to us through all his creation. Let us give thanks for these gifts. But remember to put the emphasis on the Giver, not the gift.

> Thus the heavens and the earth were completed in all their vast array. (Genesis 2:1)

March 2

"We must not rely on ourselves but on the God Who Raises the Dead"
(2 Corinthians 1:9)

I believe one of the biggest reasons why God allows trials in our lives is to remind us that he is in control. When we rely too much on our own efforts, we tend to pat ourselves on the back and envelope ourselves in

pride. Pride is one of the six things God hates (Proverbs 6:16). Despair doesn't usually show when we are full of pride. We don't show our true side when we are full of our self; we're too busy showing people what we think they want to see. When we are being who God wants us to be, we not only help ourselves but also others. It is so much easier to be free of our arrogance. That's why Jesus died for us: to set us free.

> We do not want you to be uninformed, brothers, about the hardships we suffered in the province of Asia. We were under great pressure, far beyond our ability to endure, so that we despaired even of life. Indeed, in our hearts we felt the sentence of death. But this happened that we might not rely on ourselves but on God, who raises the dead. (2 Corinthians 1:8–9)

March 3

Reverent, Submissive Trust

Reverent—honor, devotion, respect.
Submissive—yield, surrender, to commit to the decision of another.
Trust—assured reliance on the character, strength or truth of someone.

Respectfully surrender and then rely on God's character. I told my eleven-year-old nephew, Alan, that God was the only one who could never be taken away from him and to always remember that God is there to love and guide him all the days of his life. If only all young kids could receive and run with that truth and never look back or question it. Even though we all know that truth, we still take over at times and go down the wrong path. All of us are guilty of it. But God in his mercy gets us back on his path where the lights are filled with eternal oil.

> During the days of Jesus' life on earth, he offered up prayers and petitions with loud cries and tears to the one who could save him from death, and he was heard because of his reverent submission. (Hebrews 5:7)

> Trust in the Lord with all your heart and lean not on your own understanding; in all your ways acknowledge him, and he will make your paths straight. (Proverbs 3:5-6)

March 4

Look to Your Reward in Faith

But the boat was already a considerable distance from land, buffeted by the waves because the wind was against it. During the fourth watch of the night Jesus went out to them, walking on the lake. When the disciples saw him walking on the lake, they were terrified. "It's a ghost," they said, and cried out in fear. But Jesus immediately said to them, "Take courage! It is I. Do not be afraid." "Lord, if it's you," Peter replied, "tell me to come to you on the water." "Come," he said. Then Peter got down out of the boat, walked on the water and came toward Jesus. But when he saw the wind, he was afraid and, beginning to sink, cried out, "Lord, save me!" Immediately Jesus reached out his hand and caught him. "You of little faith," he said, "why did you doubt?" (Matthew 14:24–31)

Peter took his eyes off Jesus because he feared he would drown. He wasn't looking far enough ahead; all he saw was the waves. In contrast, a better example of faith would be Moses. When Moses was looking ahead to his reward, he kept his focus on God, not on his fears (Hebrews 11:24–27). Verse 27 states, "By faith, he left Egypt, not fearing the king's anger; he persevered because he saw Him who was invisible." If you're walking on the water to meet Jesus, you must keep your eyes on him. The second you realize you're walking on water you start to sink. Jesus asked Peter, "Why did you doubt?" How would you answer that question?

March 5

Trained by Discipline

Harsh consequences usually tend to teach a lesson. Hopefully, the discipline was to our disliking enough to keep us from the same act again. Some of us are quick learners, but many are not. I remember disciplining one of my sons when he was about eight or so. I slowly but surely had to take away every toy and privilege he had before he realized he wasn't having that much fun anymore. He realized I meant business and that he would have a much better day if he would just do what I asked. The same theory

works with the Lord. Obedience equals blessings and peace within. Use your discipline as hurdles to get to the finish line.

> The Lord disciplines those he loves. (Proverbs 3:12)

> Our fathers disciplined us for a little while as they thought best; but God disciplines us for our good, that we may share in his holiness. (Hebrews 12:10)

March 6

God Chooses the Terms of the Gifts He Gives

Have you figured out yet what your gift or gifts are? There are tests you can take to help you discover them. You could take the test or go straight to God in prayer and ask him to reveal your gifts. The second would be more trustworthy. It took me until I was about forty years old to finally understand what my gifts are. Of course, if I had been in the habit of listening, I would have heard God tell me over and over long ago. Your gifts are usually something you enjoy doing and are good at and are beneficial to others. It may be something that would further God's purpose. My gifts are writing, compassion for others, and giving encouragement. Seek your gifts, and be blessed as you bless others.

> Each man has his own gift from God. (1 Corinthians 7:7)

> Each one should use whatever gift he has received to serve others, faithfully administering God's grace in its various forms. (1 Peter 4:10)

March 7

Promises for Keeping the Sabbath Holy

If you keep your feet from breaking the Sabbath and from doing as you please on my holy day, if you call the Sabbath a delight and the Lord's

holy day honorable, and if you honor it by not going your own way and not doing as you please or speaking idol words, *then* you will find your joy in the Lord, and I will cause you to ride on the heights of the land and to feast on the inheritance of your father, Jacob. The mouth of the Lord has spoken. (Isaiah 58:13–14)

Wow, that's powerful, right? It can't get much clearer than that. This is a promise. Take hold of it, and share it with others. It was spoken long ago and is yours today and forever. God cannot break his promises. I like to remind him of that.

> This promise is for you and your children. (Acts 2:39)

March 8

The Error of a Moment, the Sorrow of a Lifetime

There is a young man I've known since birth who is the epitome of this truth. He didn't accept the gift of Jesus until just recently, so he grew up leaning on his own understanding and making many wrong choices. Drugs and stealing led to treatment centers, prison, and heartbreak for himself and his entire family. The biggest sorrow of his life came when he fathered an illegitimate child who was taken from him because of his lifestyle. God's grace provided a wonderful Christian couple to adopt her and to this day gives her the best of care. Although this young man visits with her from time to time, he will live out his life with the sorrow of not raising her himself. His sorrow has led to repentance and brought him to his knees before the throne of God.

> Trust in the Lord with all your heart and lean not on your own understanding. (Proverbs 3:5)

March 9

Do Not Profane Christ's Name

Ever since I started my journey of knowing Christ and made Jesus the Lord of my life, I have always wondered how to handle situations when people use his name without respect. I'm sure those taking Christ's name in vain don't even realize their blunder; it's just an empty word for them. I have noticed that people will sometimes say, "Oh, excuse me" afterward to my husband and me because they know it offends us. But my thought is, *apologize to God for using his name so disrespectfully, not to me.* I pray that God would make me bold and that the Holy Spirit would give me the words to say when this situation occurs.

Do not profane my holy name. (Leviticus 22:3)

You shall not misuse the name of the Lord your God. (Exodus 20:7)

March 10

The Lord's Grace Is Sufficient for You

Have you ever ran a relay race and passed the baton to the next runner? With all your power you do the best you can, and just when you think you can't keep up the pace, someone is there to continue for you. I relate that to how I feel when life gets so hard to bear. When I become so weak and don't feel I can face another day, the Lord takes over and reminds me that when I am weak, he is strong. He doesn't call off the race; he just takes over for a while and lets me rest. That's God's grace, always there, always sufficient, never deserved.

My grace is sufficient for you, for my power is made perfect in weakness. (2 Corinthians 12:8–9)

March 11

"We take captive every thought to make it obedient to Christ"
(2 Corinthians 10:5)

If you are finding it difficult to keep your thoughts on Jesus and the things of God, maybe the following scriptures will help.

Setting our thoughts on things above, not on earthly things. (Colossians 3:2)

Put to death whatever belongs to your earthly nature; sexual immorality, impurity, lust, evil desires and greed, which is idolatry. (Colossians 3:5)

Rid yourselves of all such things as these: anger, rage, malice, slander and filthy language from your lips. (Colossians 3:8)

Clothe yourselves with compassion, kindness, humility, gentleness and patience and forgiveness. (Colossians 3:12)

And over all these virtues, put on love, which binds them all together in perfect unity. (Colossians 3:14)

Be transformed by the renewing of your mind. (Romans 12:2)

March 12

Know the Fruit of the Holy Spirit

"Love, joy, peace, patience, kindness, goodness, faithfulness, gentleness and self- control" (Galatians 5:22). I challenge you to memorize the fruit of the Holy Spirit. Ask God every morning to fill you with them to overflowing so there isn't any room for some of the "old you" to creep back in. Write them on a 3x5 card and tape it to your bedroom or bathroom mirror. You may have heard the phrase, "I'm drinking from my saucer

because my cup has overflowed." That's where I want to be. Let all the fruit rise to the top and overflow to others. You'll be used by God for his purpose and be blessed at the same time.

Since we live by the Spirit, let us keep in step with the Spirit. (Galatians 5:25)

March 13

Submission Is Holy

If a husband and wife are living according to the will of God, it will be easy for a woman to submit to her husband if he treats her with love and respect. That is what "submit" means. It does not mean being under the iron rule of a man. Woman came from man's rib, not from his feet to be walked on or his head to be superior, but from his side to stand with him, under his arm to be protected, and next to his heart to be loved.

The wives are to be women worthy of respect, not malicious talkers but temperate and trustworthy in everything. (1 Timothy 3:11)

Husbands, love your wives just as Christ loved the church. (Ephesians 5:25)

Submit to one another out of reverence for Christ. (Ephesians 5:21)

A woman's beauty should be that of her inner self, the unfading beauty of a gentle and quiet spirit, which is of great worth in God's sight. (1 Peter 3:4)

March 14

You Can Sleep in Peace

Do you sleep well? I didn't think so; most people do not. If you do, consider yourself blessed! What is it that keeps people from a good night's sleep? Is it restlessness, stress, fear, too busy, too much caffeine, a bad mattress, decisions, worry, bad news? I guess the list could go on and on,

and you might have a few words of your own to add. *Trust* is a big word! It means you give up counting on yourself and allow God's wisdom to show you the way. A fork in the road is often detrimental. Seek God to make your paths straight and, as Proverbs 3:8 says, it will bring health to your body and nourishment to your bones. Sleep well!

> I will lie down and sleep in peace, for you alone, Lord, make me dwell in safety. (Psalm 4:8)

March 15

God Allows Obstacles to Serve His Purpose

Blessings come in all sizes, whether from the smallest of our everyday, minute decisions, to the harrowing experiences that change not only our own life but also those around us. Obstacles also come to us in all shapes and sizes; often times wrapped in glittery paper with a big red bow to get our attention; aka *temptation*. Wise is the person who seeks God's counsel when these interruptions come. We will always find obstacles in our way when God wants to change our plans to serve his purpose. But don't worry; if you decide to turn him down, he'll find someone else to do a particular job and you will have lost the blessing.

> Many are the plans of a man's heart, but it is the Lord's purpose that prevails. (Proverbs 19:21)

> Lead me on level ground. (Psalm 143:10)

March 16

God and Only God Brings Order to Spiritual Battles

In Daniel 10, we learn about answered prayer and how it is all according to God's timing, not ours. The verses talk about a time of great testing and persecution of the people of Israel and how Daniel's prayer for help

seemed to go unanswered. It says the angel, Gabriel, was detained for several weeks on his journey to help Daniel because of interference from the evil one. God sent Michael, another angel, to help Gabriel in this spiritual battle. So many things are going on in the heavens of which we have no understanding. Satan and his angels cause much mischief within the church and God's people, but we can rejoice that Christ and his angels act on our behalf. God hears our prayer the instant we send it up to him, but there are times when our answers are delayed because God is putting spiritual chaos in order. Remember, delay is not denial.

> Wait for the Lord; be strong and take heart and wait for the Lord. (Psalm 27:14)

March 17

Never Give Up, Never Give In

It's been said, "If you don't stand for something, you will fall for anything." It's really a great feeling to know you have persevered to the bitter end. That's where you collect your blessing. Sometimes the last key turns the lock and opens the door. If you ask that person one more time to come to church with you, and the answer is yes, you both win! You've done the planting. Now let the Holy Spirit do the watering, and wait for the harvest. Nothing good from the Lord is easy to attain, but through him all things are possible.

> Let us not become weary in doing good, for at the proper time we will reap a harvest if we do not give up. (Galatians 6:9)

> Blessed is the man who perseveres. (James 1:12)

March 18

Be Holy

These are Jesus' words, not mine! I'm still trying to figure this one out. It must only be by faith that this could possibly happen, right? So if we muster

up enough faith to be holy, we will be holy. Is that it? Just how much faith would we need? When I found these scriptures, I had a great peace come over me. In Leviticus 20:24, God told the Israelites through Moses that he himself is the one who makes us holy. God says he has set us apart from the nations and has given us his Ten Commandments to help us be holy. Know them and know your God intimately. And remember, he didn't give us the Ten Commandments because he thought we could keep them. He knew we would have trouble with that and would seek him for help. And note: they are called the Ten Commandments, not the Ten Suggestions.

> Consecrate yourself and be holy, because I am the Lord your God. Keep my decrees and follow them. I am the Lord who makes you holy. (Leviticus 20:7–8)

> You are to be holy to me because I, the Lord, am holy, and I have set you apart from the nations to be my own. (Leviticus 20:26)

March 19

Maintain a Holy Composure of Spirit

Keep looking straight ahead, focused on Jesus, and don't look back as Lot's wife did in the city of Sodom. They were warned by God's angels to not look back when they left the city as it was being destroyed. When Lot's wife looked back, God turned her into a pillar of salt. She did not persevere or put her trust in the Lord and thus lost her composure. We must not only read God's word. We must also do what it says. Otherwise, what is the point? When we read, we receive it intellectually, but "to do" is to receive it in our heart. Then we receive his blessings and are able to maintain our walk with him. His Holy Spirit will guide us through the difficult times, and we will be able to rejoice in the Lord, no matter what.

> That is why, for Christ's sake, I delight in weaknesses, in insults, in hardships, persecution, and difficulties. For when I am weak, then I am strong. (2 Corinthians 12:8–10)

> Do not be overcome by evil but overcome evil with good. (Romans 12:21)

March 20

A Young Man's Prayer

So many young men today are tempted with things like infidelity, pornography, incest, and other ungodly ways. Even those who appear righteous and walking with the Lord are not beyond temptation and have at times given in. Is it because they believe the lies from Satan more than they believe God's word? When a man is seeking God with all his heart and desiring to live in God's will, he will not part from God's protection. That is God's promise, and we can rely on it. If we have the mind of Christ, our thinking will not lead us to these detestable ways and we will be free. That's been God's plan from the very beginning. He has made a way for us to walk in his truth.

Set your mind on things above, not on earthly things. (Colossians 3:2)

Do not conform any longer to the pattern of this world, but be transformed by the renewing of your mind. Then you will be able to test and approve what God's will is; his good, pleasing and perfect will. (Romans 12:2)

March 21

Jesus Knows Who Will Betray Him or Believe in Him

Don't ever try to fool God. He knows every angle of our manipulations. He knows our words of betrayal far before we even think about saying them. God's heart is so tender toward us. If you have something in your heart that would prove some form of unbelief, let it go. Give it to God today. He's expecting it, you know. He will take it, reshape it, wrap it with a huge bow, and send it back to you as truth. All he wants is your love and faith in him. He provides everything else—unconditionally.

For Jesus had known from the beginning which of them did not believe and who would betray him. (John 6:64)

Then you will know the truth and the truth will set you free. (John 8:32)

March 22

You Will No Doubt Have Trials and Tribulation

We have trials so we do not depend on ourselves but on God who raises the dead. Also, our experiences may help others who are going through similar trials. Many times, our trials are the very footsteps to our victory. Always ask God what he wants you to learn from your experience. He has allowed the trial to give you the grace to know him better and to help you grow in your faith because, ultimately, he wants you to pass it on. That's how he uses us to build his kingdom. Always be watchful!

> Let us then approach the throne of grace with confidence, so that we may receive mercy and find grace to help us in our time of need. (Hebrews 4:16)

> Therefore we do not lose heart. Though outwardly we are wasting away, yet inwardly we are being renewed day by day. For our light and momentary troubles are achieving for us an eternal glory that far outweighs them all. So we fix our eyes not on what is seen, but on what is unseen. For what is seen is temporary, but what is unseen is eternal. (2 Corinthians 4:16–18)

March 23

Charging God with Wrongdoing

No one suffered more than Job. Yet even though his friends and family told him to curse God, he praised God instead. He didn't ask why. I'm not sure

I would have the extreme faith that Job portrayed. His home, livestock, and even children were taken. He was so distraught that his closest friends could not recognize him. He never indulged in a pity party. That gets you nowhere. Hopefully, you will read Job's story and learn from it. The value of praising God is limitless. We limit ourselves. So many stories in the Bible refer to the perseverance of God's people and how God used them to further his kingdom. Once you go through it and look back on your circumstances, pain, and doubt, you will see the fruit of your labor. God gave us the book of Job to help us understand God's character and that we should accept the bad along with the good. God never makes mistakes, and his answers are never too late. His timing is not our timing. His grace is always sufficient. So if you are in the midst of a pity party, stand up, brush yourself off, and start all over again—with God walking in front of you, not behind.

"Naked I came from my mother's womb, and naked I will depart."
The Lord gave and the Lord has taken away; may the name of the Lord be praised. (Job 1:21–22)

March 24

Jesus Used Scripture against Satan

If Jesus quoted scripture at Satan, how much more do we need to do so? We need to be on the defense at all times because Satan is alive and doesn't scare easily. Satan may not be afraid of us, but he despises the authority we have over him in Jesus' name. Jesus also gave us the example of fasting and praying. He says, "*When* you fast," not "*if* you fast." I have to admit I lack the discipline to fast. However, I know that taking authority over Satan in the mighty name of Jesus works—every time. You don't need to scream at Satan. Gently remind him that you are a child of the King and that you have total authority over him. Sing praises to God and Satan will leave.

Jesus said to him, "Away from me, Satan! For it is written: 'Worship the Lord your God, and serve him only.'" Then the devil left him, and angels came and attended him. (Matthew 4:10–11)

March 25

We Can Ask God for Healing

Do you doubt that God heals? Do you pray for healing and expect it to happen? There are so many scriptures concerning healing. Yes, God is in the business of healing, even today. However, we must pray with an attitude of praise and thanksgiving and refrain from becoming angry or discouraged when his answer is different from ours. We can pray for a miracle. God says to pray unceasingly. But when we pray, the prayer needs to end in, "Thy will be done." It's difficult to get those last few words to roll off our tongue. Before going to the cross, when Jesus was in the garden of Gethsemane on the Mount of Olives, he asked God to take away his agonizing suffering but ended his request with, "Yet not as I will, but Thy will be done" (Matthew 26:39). If God is using your trial to help the world in some way, be thankful that he finds you worthy to use. And keep praying for those miracles. When you seek his will before yours, you will be blessed!

Take heart, your faith has healed you. (Matthew 9:22)

He heals the broken hearted and binds up their wounds. (Psalm 147:3)

March 26

The Reward of Obedience Is Always Worth the Sacrifice

The best example to confirm this statement would be Jesus' obedience to his Father. If Jesus hadn't been obedient, neither you nor I would be where we are today. There would have been no resurrection or ascension. When we die, our bodies would just rot in the ground and the hope of seeing our loved ones again would be in vain. Any sacrifice we suffer through obedience to God is always worth it and will always bring forth good somewhere down the line—for his glory. Always remember, if God brings you to it, he will bring you through it, and you will receive a blessing that will benefit you and perhaps change someone else's life. Most times

it is inconceivable what God has planned for you. That's why it's called walking in faith.

> Jesus replied, "Blessed are those who hear the word of God and obey it." (Luke 11:28)

March 27

Talk to Your Children about the Things of the Lord

Jesus first started preaching in the temple in Jerusalem at the feast of the Passover when he was only twelve years of age. It was his mission to tell people about himself and God. Now he has commissioned us to tell others. Our biggest challenge is to bring up our children to know, love, and serve the Lord. To know that your children are walking in the truth will bring great joy and peace for them and for you. There is evidence of God everywhere. Just pick one of his blessings and talk heart to heart with your children about them. Let them know that even they are evidence that there is a loving God. And they will teach their children, and they will teach their children, and so on, and so on.

> I have no greater joy than to know my children are walking in the truth. (3 John 4)

March 28

Pray for Things Promised

The definition of *promise* is 1) a pledge to do or not to do something specified, and 2) a reason for expectation for success or improvement.

It seems as we grow spiritually, we also grow in the manner in which we pray. I find myself praying more in the way Jesus teaches us to pray in the Lord's Prayer—according to God's will. Matthew 18:20 says, "When two or three come together in my name, there I am also." If God is with us,

who can be against us? When you pray within the boundaries of God, I believe it's all right to remind God of his promises—not because he has forgotten but because you are holding him to them. He cannot and will not break his promises. Ask and then expect great things!

> Again, I tell you that if two or more of you on earth agree about anything you ask for, it will be done for you by my Father in Heaven. (Matthew 18:19)

> Because God wanted to make the unchanging nature of his purpose very clear to the heirs of what was promised, he confirmed it with an oath. (Hebrews 6:17)

March 29

Am I Impacting People for Eternity?

When we are living in God's will and loving him above all else, we will obey his command to bear fruit. "Bearing fruit" means to give what we have received from God to the rest of the world. We don't have to put forth effort to bear fruit; it will happen through our obedience and the work of the Holy Spirit. Jesus explains in John 15 that he is the true vine and we are the branches. God is the gardener, and he prunes the branches in order to produce more fruit. Our fruit is then given out to the world—that gets life from the same vine—all for God's purpose and glory. Praise God!

> You did not choose me, but I chose you and appointed you to go and bear fruit—fruit that will last. Then the Father will give you whatever you ask in my name. (John 15:16)

> Freely you have received; freely give. (Matthew 10:8)

March 30

Jesus Comes to Heal; the Devil comes to Destroy

Have you ever been in bondage? Bondage is something that keeps you from knowing the truth. Are you in a situation like that at this very moment? Believing a lie will keep you from knowing the truth. It could keep you from experiencing all that God wants for you. Holding a grudge could cause you and others great pain. Since the devil is the father of all lies, he enjoys keeping us tightly bound like an octopus crushing his prey. Only one thing can remove the stronghold—knowing Christ and believing in his word, the Bible. Jesus used scripture to crush Satan's power, and we can do the same. "Know the truth and truth shall set you free" (John 8:32). *Free*—that's a great word, isn't it?

For he is a liar and the father of all lies. (John 8:44)

March 31

Canonization Does Not Make a Saint

Some churches make a big deal out of canonizing a person long after his or her death. The book of Acts describes a saint as a spiritual worker. A saint is a person who is still alive and has done Christ's work on earth most of his or her life. Mother Teresa, for example, lived in Calcutta and fed the poor and helped the sick her entire life, never expecting anything in return. God blessed her with old age, health, courage, strength, and perseverance—all for his glory. Everything he gave her, she gave away to someone else. Mother Teresa is just one example of many people that God used while on earth. They were saints in God's eyes.

Paul went to visit the saints. (Acts 9:32)

Precious in the sight of the Lord is the death of his saints. (Psalm 116:15)

April 1

Holy Boldness

"Everyone who calls on the name of the Lord will be saved" (Romans 10:13). It goes on to say, "How then can they call on the one they have not believed in? How can they believe in the one of whom they have not heard? And how can they hear without someone preaching to them? And how can they preach unless they are sent?" (Romans 10:14-15). We are commissioned by Christ to preach the good news of the gospel. I don't always feel adequate to follow through with that command. However, I pray, asking the Holy Spirit to give me boldness, and I find myself speaking only the words he leads me to say. God doesn't look for those who are adequate, only for those who are willing.

> Now Lord, enable your servant to speak your word with great boldness. (Acts 4:29)

> How beautiful are the feet of those who bring good news. (Romans 10:15)

April 2

You Reap according to Your Faith

In the gospel of Matthew, two blind men follow Jesus, asking for his mercy. Jesus asks them, "Do you believe that I am able to do this?" After they say yes, he touches their eyes and says, "According to your faith it will be done to you" (Matthew 9:29). And their sight was restored. Even though we don't experience many miraculous healings and don't always seem to have enough faith, remember that we have a real big God who will grant us strength and faith to believe, if we will just ask (Philippians 4:13). Remember, when we are weak, he is strong. Ask him for a strong faith so you can reap the harvest that is available to you. For everyone who asks receives; he who seeks finds; and to him who knocks, the door will be opened. (Matthew 7:8)

April 3

Abandoned to the Holy Ghost

Abandoned to the Holy Ghost means relinquishing all others to surrender to a higher power. I wonder why it takes us so long to surrender our lives to the Holy Spirit. Why don't we feel his presence more often? Could it be there is a spirit of doubt or fear within us? Do we think our way could possibly be better? Jesus gave us the Holy Spirit as a guide and a comforter. We need to trust in God's ways and his plan for us but not on our own, lest we stumble and fall. We need to use Jesus as our ever-present helper and remember that he has overcome the world. If Jesus gave us the Holy Spirit to guide, direct, protect, and care for us, whom shall we fear? Surrender today. Do it now and your life will be all God intends it to be.

Help me overcome my unbelief. (Mark 9:24)

Trust in the Lord with all your heart and lean not on your own understanding; in all your ways acknowledge him, and he will make your paths straight. (Proverbs 3:5)

April 4

He Who Suffers Most Has Most to Give

If we can't share in his suffering, we won't see the joy in his glory. Christ showed us to what extent a human can suffer. Of course, our sufferings would never reach the point of sweating blood like Jesus did. By his death, he gave everlasting life for all mankind. We do not have to be afraid to suffer. Suffering always builds character, and after that, we are prepared to help others who are passing the same way. After the rain, comes the rainbow—another one of God's promises. Be a rainbow in someone else's cloud.

So then, those who suffer according to God's will should commit themselves to their faithful Creator and continue to do good. (1 Peter 4:19)

I have set my rainbow in the clouds, and it will be the sign of the covenant between me and the earth. (Genesis 9:13)

April 5

"Give to Caesar what is Caesar's and to God what is God's"
(Matthew 22:21)

You realize, of course, that everything belongs to God: your money, assets, abilities, and body. Through any good circumstance, God has allowed you to earn or be gifted any money you might have. Therefore, as thankful stewards, we should take heed to what the Bible says regarding it. We pay our tithe, 10 percent, to God before the government takes its share. We pay our bills, put a little something away for a rainy day and/or retirement, and then we live within our means. God promises blessings for tithing; he even says to test him on this! If you can let go of your money, you will notice how your desires will line up with his. Let go and let God. It's so much easier.

You can't serve both God and money. (Matthew 6:24)

Be still and know that I am God; I will be exalted among the nations, I will be exalted in the earth. (Psalm 46:10)

April 6

Hospitality Is a Gift from God

Billy Graham's daily devotional talks about a man who was spending the night at a friend's home. As the guest was turning in, his friend turned to him and said, "Let me know if you need anything and I'll show you how to do without it." If your gift is hospitality, remember to ask God who he wants you to bless. You never know who your kindness will touch and how it will change a person's life. You never know when an act of kindness

could possibly bring a person to Christ. Your gift was given to you so you could pass it on.

Freely you have received, freely give. (Matthew 10:8)

Give and it will be given unto you. A good measure, pressed down, shaken together and running over, will be poured into your lap. For with the measure you use, it will be measured to you. (Luke 6:38)

April 7

Jesus Intercedes for Us

We stumble, we hurt, and we cry, until we realize all we need to do is put Jesus first in our life. The scriptures below state that Jesus prayed to his Father for our sake. The gospel of John is full of Jesus' teachings and prayers for us. God heard and answered every one of them according to Jesus' asking and according to our own needs. He is the bread that came down from heaven (John 6:41). Let him nourish you!

In Hebrews 7:25, he intercedes for us.
In Luke 22:32, he prays for weak believers.
In Luke 23:34, he asks God to forgive us.
In John 14:16, he asks God to give us the Holy Spirit.
In John 17:9, he prays for us because God gave us to Jesus.

April 8

God Doesn't Remove Us from Hardships
He Helps Us through Them

Even though we don't want to go through hardships, they help build our character. We can't always expect things to go our way, saying, "It's my way or the highway." We need to pray, persevere, and press on. Wrapped in God's peace is the way to travel on your journey. You can try it on your

own, but for the best outcome, you need to give Jesus the reigns. God knows all the back roads you will take. He sees the bridges to be crossed, the mountains to be climbed, and the snares in the dark set for you. You may be destined to go that route, but you might as well hold his hand tightly and let him lead you to the Promised Land. It is better to walk in the dark with God than in the light without him.

> My grace is sufficient for you. (2 Corinthians 12:7–10)

> This is the way; walk in it. (Isaiah 30:21)

April 9

Satan Rushes While God's Spirit Gently Leads

Have you ever made a quick decision and gone ahead without consulting God? A deal looks good, and without giving any thought that it could be a temptation, we get involved hook, line, and sinker. When we finally see our blunder, realizing we not only hurt ourselves in the process but also others, we wonder why we acted so quickly and selfishly. God gave us the Holy Spirit as a helper, a comforter, and a guide in all truth. Always seek him first. Wisdom and knowledge are the first things we need before stepping out. Wisdom is knowing what to do, and knowledge is knowing how to do it.

> Seek first his kingdom and his righteousness and all these things will be given to you as well. (Matthew 6:33)

> But when he, the Spirit of truth, comes, he will guide you into all truth. (John 16:13)

April 10

All That Is Necessary for Evil to Triumph Is for Good People to Do Nothing
… Edmund Burke

Here are ten things we can do to triumph over evil:

1. Speak up when we see someone being mistreated.
2. Vote for godly people.
3. Correct a wrong belief.
4. Don't be involved in a bad plan.
5. Confront sin.
6. Turn in a thief.
7. Spread the gospel.
8. Pray before going out into the day.
9. Persevere to victory.
10. Obey God's Ten Commandments.

> Turn from evil and do good; seek peace and pursue it. (Psalm 34:14)

April 11

God Expects a Response for His Grace

Grace is receiving something we don't deserve. What would be the best response to God's grace, that is, if we realize it as grace and receive it? Thankfulness, praise, humility, repentance, and obedience are just a few things that come to mind. But some people are too proud to accept God's grace. They don't recognize it because they are too busy believing they don't need any help while others feel they don't deserve it. If you are rejecting grace or any other gift from God, you need to get your eyes off yourself and focus on the one who formed you in your mother's womb. He is the epitome of grace. You need to acknowledge it and be thankful.

> I do not set aside the grace of God, for if righteousness could be gained through the law, Christ died for nothing. (Galatians 2:21)

April 12

Sorrow Comes to Create Spaces
in the Heart for Joy

Sorrow is caused by an abundance of distinct circumstances: a loved one's death or separation from that person, oppression that seems irrevocable, or simply not feeling the presence of God in your life. The book of James talks about finding joy in our sorrow because sorrow can produce perseverance, which leads to finding God through our troubles. Walking in God's truth produces joy. It seems that sorrow and joy are tied together, similar to that of a tapestry. The tangled threads on the back of the tapestry allow for a beautiful image on the front. We actually need sorrow to experience joy. Think back to when God created the balance in your life. And who through your sorrow has found God, creating yet another beautiful tapestry?

> Consider it pure joy, my brothers, whenever you face trials of many kinds, because you know that the testing of your faith develops perseverance. (James 1:2)

> I tell you the truth, you will weep and mourn while the world rejoices. You will grieve, but your grief will turn to joy. (John 16:20)

April 13

Jesus Was a Blue-Collar Worker

Jesus worked diligently for his Father. He didn't wear a suit. Nor did he sit behind a beautiful mahogany desk. His wages were low and benefits were hardly worth mentioning. His lunch breaks were short, and a vacation was something he never dreamed about. He was what you would call a blue-collar worker. The job he was put on earth to do, however, was not of monetary value. I'm not addressing his carpentry job, for which I am sure he was greatly recognized. I'm talking about his daily routine that consisted of gathering as many people as he could to love and teach about his Father. While thousands sat on a hillside intently listening to him and full of wonder, others spit in his face and rejected him. He worked without

restraint, and at the end of a long and strenuous day, like any other human, he was exhausted. He ate and slept and then got up the next day to do the same thing all over again in obedience to his Father. At the end of his young life, while suffering a most horrendous death on the cross for our sake, he asked his Father to forgive the very ones who were pounding the nails. Now he sits at God's right hand. Hard work always pays off. Blood, sweat, and tears never really keep anyone down.

> Whatever you do, work at it with all your heart, as working for the Lord, not for men. (Colossians 3:23)

April 14

God and I

When Jesus walked this earth, he was totally human and essentially dependent on his Father. He believed that God was preparing him for a ministry of denying himself to save the entire world. Do you think this was difficult for Jesus to understand? The bible tells us he spent a lot of time in seclusion with his Father, talking with him; just himself and the Almighty One. Jesus felt the need of perfect solitude and used it as an example of how our days should be; a time set aside for just you and God. Jesus had much more to deal with than any of us. If he took time to search the Father's thoughts, we should too. You need some "God and I" time. Seek him, desire to know him and he will show himself to you. Let the rest of the world deal with itself. Be still, and know that he is God.

Be still and know that I am God; I will be exalted among the nations, I will be exalted in the earth. (Psalm 46:10)

April 15

To be Blessed Is to be Made
Happy by God's Goodness

God's goodness comes in many small, mysterious packages throughout our lives. At times we may be afraid to open the package because of its

unknown content. To set a package aside means to lose that blessing. There are probably many beautifully boxed blessings on a shelf somewhere in heaven for the simple reason our arms weren't open to receive them. Whether they are spiritual blessings or physical blessings, they come from God's goodness. Your happiness is in his hands. Look for his blessings. They're everywhere!

> I will sing to the Lord for he has been good to me. (Psalm 13:6)

> A happy heart makes the face cheerful, but heartache crushes the spirit. (Proverbs 15:13)

April 16

We Are Not the Judge of the Scriptures; The Scriptures Judge Us

The value of God's words in the Bible goes far beyond our finite understanding. We can find the answer to every single question we have about life, death, and all that is layered in between. The scriptures give only absolute truths, so don't take anyone's word for it; ask God yourself to show you why you should believe in him. When you know the truth it can set you free. Free to be all that God has created you to be.

> All scripture is God breathed and is useful for teaching, rebuking, correcting and training in righteousness so that the man of God may be thoroughly equipped for every good work. (2 Timothy 3:16–17)

> Then you will know the truth and the truth will set you free. (John 8:32)

April 17

Don't Fear Losing What Is Not Meant to Be

God has had a plan for us since before the world began. He not only knew us but also loved us while you were yet in our mother's womb. If he knit us together himself, why do we fight to keep the things that are not in his plan for us?

He knows best and is in control so don't argue with him. Instead, by faith, surrender your will to him, not knowing what lies ahead. Why gain everything else but lose the very thing God wants you to have? The greatness of knowing Christ and having a personal relationship with him far outweighs anything else you might feel you want or deserve. Even though we don't deserve anything, Jesus died to give us everything. Open your heart and hands and let go of all that tempts you to live in your own desires. Let go and let God. And enjoy!

> I consider everything a loss compared to the surpassing greatness of knowing Christ Jesus my Lord, for whose sake I have lost all things. (Philippians 3:8)

> What good is it for a man to gain the whole world, yet lose his very self. (Luke 9:25)

April 18

Eternal Glory Far Outweighs
Our Earthly Trouble

When Jesus was in the garden of Gethsemane (Matthew 26:36–39), he looked up to his Father in heaven and prayed, "Take this cup from me, but your will not mine be done." God seemed to answer, "What is to come next far outweighs the situation you are now in." God knows our circumstances and is never surprised by what takes place in our lives. He just says, "My grace is sufficient for you" (2 Corinthians 12:9). If God's grace was sufficient for Jesus, who was just as human as we are, it must

be sufficient for us. One of my favorite songs, Turn your eyes upon Jesus by Helen H. Lemmel, says, "Turn your eyes upon Jesus, look straight in his wonderful face and the things of earth will grow strangely dim in the light of his glory and grace." So next time you experience an overwhelming situation, reach for God's abundant grace. Know it is enough for you and that the mansion he is building for you is well worth the wait (John 14:2).

> Therefore we do not lose heart. Though outwardly we are wasting away, yet inwardly we are being renewed day by day. For our light and momentary troubles are achieving for us an eternal glory that far outweighs them all. (2 Corinthians 4:16–18)

> Let us fix our eyes on Jesus. (Hebrews 12:2)

April 19

Chaos Reminds Us We Are Not in Control

September 11, 2001, was the epitome of chaos. The morning started out as a routinely beautiful day, and New York City residents were bustling about as usual. However, what began as an uneventful day turned on them without any notice, and the entire city was thrown upside down as disorder and confusion spilled into the streets and the lives of thousands of people, some never to be seen again. Everyone was out of control, including the emergency teams. Not only was there a gaping hole in the middle of New York City, there were also gashes in the hearts of those injured and of those who had loved ones dying in their arms. The chaos was felt all around the world. Only God could foresee the trouble coming that morning, but this attack was not a surprise to him. Prayers went up, and he came down to gather the survivors in his arms. He healed them and let them go, again hoping for a new response to his grace. I think God was tugging on many people's hearts that day, saying, "Can you see me? Can you hear me?" Don't wait for a tragedy to realize you are not in control. We think we have so much going on in our lives. Let God be in control, and you will deal with much less stress.

> Be still and know that I am God. (Psalm 46:10)

April 20

God Knows Us before We Are Born

God knows all about us. He knows the decisions we will make and the heartbreaks we will suffer. He knows the whole story, including the last chapter. From beginning to end, his love for us remains the same. We fall down; he picks us up. We sin; he forgives. We suffer; he heals. We lose our life; he gives us a new one. Psalm 139:16 says, "Your eyes saw my unformed body. All the days ordained for me were written in your book before one of them came to be." God is familiar with all our ways and knows our every thought and desire. We can't hide from him. His hand is ever guiding and his eyes ever watchful. Repent and let his Holy Spirit lead you on level ground (Psalm 143:10).

> For you created my inmost being; you knit me together in my mother's womb. (Psalm 139:13)

April 21

We don't have to be Perfect, Just Willing

Has the Lord ever asked you to do something for him and you immediately skipped over it, believing you were unqualified? Usually, the Holy Spirit will gently nudge you, but when the nudge becomes a firm hand on your shoulder, you need to look up and say, "Here I am, Lord." In Exodus 4, when God gave Moses the task of leading the Israelites out of Egypt, Moses pleaded with the Lord to find someone else who would do a better job. Moses said, "What if they don't listen to me? I am slow of speech." God responded, "Who gave man his mouth? Who makes him deaf or mute? Who gives him sight or makes him blind? Is it not I, the Lord?" (Exodus 4:1-16). At times, we need reminding that God will never give us a task without first giving us the grace to complete it. When you step out of your comfort zone and agree to what he asks of you, you will be blessed. Your fear will become less than your desire to please him.

> He that started a good work in you will be faithful to complete it. (Philippians 1:6)

April 22

Don't Settle for Less than
What God Wants to Give

Even though at times you have very little faith, you need to realize that you have a great big God and he has big plans for you. I'm sure you've seen the picture of Jesus standing outside the closed door with his hand outstretched to open it. Have you ever noticed that there is no doorknob? It can only be opened from the inside—where you are. He will never cross the threshold without your permission. He waits patiently but intently to be invited in. He is knocking. Get up, go to the door, and answer it! Allow him entrance into your inner chamber. He wants to give himself to you.

> For everyone who asks, receives; he who seeks finds; and to him who knocks, the door will be opened. (Matthew 7:8)

April 23

The Peril of an Empty Heart

To me, an empty heart would be the absence of love, void of anything good and barely beating. It sounds extremely sad, doesn't it? I believe we all have a small, empty space in our hearts waiting to be filled only by God. He put the space there and also the desire within us to fill the space with him. Through his death on the cross and our acceptance of his gift of salvation, the space is filled with his love and goodness. Nothing of the world can keep our heart filled. The world is like a blank page. Only God's word can fill us. Are you hungry for it? Remember, if the Holy Spirit is the doorman to your heart, only good will enter.

> Listen to my words and keep them within your heart, for they are life to those who find them and health to a man's whole body ... Guard your heart for it is the wellspring of Life. (Proverbs 4:20, 23)

April 24

Jesus' Coming Fulfilled the Old Testament Prophecies

The New Testament fulfills the prophecies about Jesus' coming. When you study the Bible and allow God to infiltrate your mind with how the Old Testament and New Testament intertwine, you will see a brilliant tapestry that is awesome to comprehend. No human being could ever claim to have written such a complex story with such a simple message. All scripture is inspired by God. When you read the Bible, you can be assured that what you read is exactly what God wants you to know. Each person who wrote a book of the Bible was inspired by God about what to write. It's a good book. It's been on the best-seller list for centuries! If you love history, you'll love studying these books. And you'll fall in love with the main Character!

> All scripture is God-breathed and is useful for teaching, rebuking, correcting and training in righteousness, so that the man of God may be thoroughly equipped for every good work. (2 Timothy 3:16–17)

April 25

Think Positive

Jesus' red-letter words in the Bible are a great example of positive thinking. He spoke in parables and answered many questions submitted to him with a question. He stuck to the facts and spoke only the truth. Jesus said, "Know the truth and the truth will set you free" (John 8:32). You can check out or buy books about thinking positive, but the best way to have a positive attitude is to receive the mind of Christ and be led to all truth through his Holy Spirit. When we remain focused on Jesus, the author of life, we will have that little God-shaped hole in our heart filled with his red-letter truths. Then the negativity will positively be overcome.

> Set your mind on things above not on early things. (Colossians 3:2)

Finally, brothers, whatever is true, whatever is noble, whatever is right, whatever is pure, whatever is lovely, whatever is admirable - if anything is excellent or praiseworthy - think on these things. Whatever you have learned or received or heard from me, or seen in me - put it into practice. And the God of peace will be with you. (Philippians 4:8–9)

April 26

We Are Responsible to Vote for
Those with Biblical Moral Values

One of the best ways we can give back to God is by honoring our privilege to vote. We must have leaders in place who will veto the things that would not further God's kingdom. We must uphold our Constitution and God's Ten Commandments. Be bold. Speak out against abortion and uphold God's definition of marriage, which is between one man and one woman. A billboard puts this into perspective: "When we forget that our country is one nation under God, we will be a nation gone under." (Quote by Ronald Reagan.) Stand up for your principles, and be bold for the sake of Christ and all the world. If you don't stand for something, you will fall for anything.

> Give to Caesar what is Caesar's and to God what is God's. (Matthew 22:21)

April 27

The Bible Is a Mirror to Your Soul

Come to me all you who are weary and burdened, and I will give you rest. Take my yoke upon you and learn from me, for I am gentle and humble in heart, and you will find rest for your souls. For my yoke is easy and my burden is light. (Matthew 11:28–30)

This is Jesus talking to *you*!

Do you realize you are daily infused with his grace whether you deserve it or not? He is omnipresent, which means he is present in all places at all times. He is omnipotent, which means he has unlimited power and that nothing you do surprises him. You need to grasp the concept that he loves you unconditionally and that no act on your part will keep his grace from you. Grace is unmerited help. That means we don't deserve it but because of Jesus, all things are restored. Love and value yourself; God invested a great deal in you.

> Thanks be to God! He gives us the victory through our Lord, Jesus Christ. (1 Corinthians 15:57)

April 28

"Though He Slay Me, Yet Will I Hope in Him"

(Job 13:15)

When you were just a child, your parents disciplined you because they loved you and wanted to protect you from things of the world. They helped you in your decision-making and hopefully encouraged you in the Lord's ways. Your heavenly Father does the very same thing. He disciplines you to gain your trust and for you to return his love. He wants his will to become your desire. Don't lose faith when things appear to be a mess. You need to continue to trust in him and in him alone. He will lead you on level ground (Psalm 143:10).

> Teach me to do your will, for you are my God; may your good Spirit lead me on level ground. (Psalm 143:10)

> My son, do not make light of the Lord's discipline, and do not lose heart when he rebukes you, because the Lord disciplines those he loves, and he punishes everyone he accepts as a son. (Hebrews 12:5–6)

April 29

When You Go through Trials, You Are in His Shadow

When I first became a Christian, one of the many books I saturated myself with was *Power in Praise* by Merlin Carothers. It was a great book about praising God when in the midst of trouble or sorrow. It took me quite some time to understand that concept. I learned I wasn't actually thanking God for putting me in the situation but thanking and praising him for going through it with me as he allowed it to unfold. He saw the situation and walked me *through* it rather than *around* it so I could grow in character and perseverance and love for him. It is always better to walk in the dark with God than in the light without him.

> Consider it pure joy my brothers, whenever you face trials of many kinds, because you know that the testing of your faith develops perseverance. Perseverance must finish its work so that you may be mature and complete, not lacking anything. (James 1:2–4)

April 30

Lodge God in Your Soul

Open the door, invite God in, and make him a permanent tenant in your heart. Give him the best room you have. Get to know him, and listen to his many parables. Show him your innermost self and allow a relationship to form. Tuck him deep into the core of your soul. Fill yourself totally with him so there is no room for anything but the Holy Spirit. Jesus says in Matthew, "Come to me and I will give you rest." Everything Jesus says to you is in the form of a promise and it will not be broken. He is faithful and true. You can consider it a gentleman's handshake.

> Here I am—I stand at the door and knock. (Revelation 3:20)

Come to me, all you who are weary and burdened, and I will give you rest. Take my yoke upon you and learn from me, for I am gentle and humble in heart, and you will find rest for your souls. For my yoke is easy and my burden is light. (Matthew 11:28—30)

May 1

Let God Reveal His Son in You

In Matthew and Second Peter we read about the day Jesus came from Galilee to the Jordan River to be baptized. John the Baptist performed baptisms on every person who traveled from Jerusalem, Judea, and all of Jordan. But when Jesus came into the water, John felt unworthy to do the job and humbly said to Jesus, "I need to be baptized by you, and do you come to me?" (Matthew 3:14). The heavens immediately opened and the Spirit of God came down as a dove and landed on Jesus. A voice from heaven said, "This is my son, whom I love; with him I am well pleased" (Matthew 3:16-17). After hearing God speak, John readily consented and baptized Jesus (Matthew 3:15). This was God introducing his son to you. Now it's time for you to consent to Jesus' probing and let God reveal himself in you. You may be feeling unworthy, but that's the reason Jesus came. Let go and let God.

This is my Son in whom I am well pleased. (Matthew 3:17; 2 Peter 1:17)

May 2

"Let Not Your Heart be Troubled"
(John 14:27)

God reminded me of this verse one day when my heart was so heavy I didn't even know how to pray and it has given me great encouragement many times since. These are red-letter words spoken by Jesus to his disciples a few days before he was arrested and crucified. He spoke about giving us his peace and that he would send his Holy Spirit to comfort and lead us. We are the blessed recipients of God's kindness through his Son, Jesus. Don't ever feel like you are alone in your troubles. You have the Holy Trinity, Father, Son, and Holy Spirit, on your side. A cord of three strands is not quickly broken (Ecclesiastes 4:12).

May 3

Only God Has the Power to
Transform a Heart

Not only are we incapable of transforming our heart, we also don't know what is wrong with it or why it needs to change. Our heart is the part of us that God wants, and when he has it, everything else will follow. Ask God to search your heart and see if there is anything he wants to change in you. If you ask him, he will show you, so be ready and willing to listen and obey. More often than not, transformation of any degree is a process; it doesn't happen in one day. God will never give up on you and will never leave you or forsake you. That's a promise!

> I will give you a new heart and put a new spirit in you; I will remove from you your heart of stone and give you a heart of flesh. (Ezekiel 36:26)

> Create in me a pure heart, O God, and renew a steadfast spirit within me. (Psalm 51:10)

May 4

Be Unshakable No Matter What

Being unshakable would probably take some practice, don't you think? When something in my life is so out of sync that I fear even God can't intervene, I try to recall previous situations when he showed up, sometimes at the very last minute, and saved the day. That's how he strengthens your faith—by letting you wait on him. Get your strength from the power of his word. Don't lean on your own understanding about any situation. Be bold and wait on him. Delay is not denial.

> Now, Lord, consider their threats and enable your servants to speak your word with great boldness. (Acts 4:29)

When I called, you answered me; you made me bold and stouthearted. (Psalm 138:3)

May 5

The Deceitfulness of Our Ego

This is such a powerful statement. Doesn't it make sense that our ego would lie to us? When we are self-centered, there is no room for God—or anyone else for that matter. We build up our ego because it is a self-sustaining mechanism to survive low confidence or self-esteem. It's a slippery slope because arrogance ultimately follows. It takes brokenness to be rid of pride. It takes putting on the full armor of God every morning and letting God take control of our lives. Then our faith will be in him rather than in ourselves. We will be humbled, and our souls will be restored.

Pride goes before destruction, a haughty spirit before a fall. (Proverbs 16:18)

May 6

False Security

We can certainly see from the recent collapse of our economy that none of us should take financial security for granted. On the other hand, God's hand, we have his promises to hold firmly in our hearts. Hebrews 6:18 says, "It is impossible for God to lie." This hope is an anchor for our soul, firm and secure (Hebrew 6:19). Having God as our anchor allows us to stand steady, rely on his promises, and eventually arrive at the Promised Land. And like Abraham, after waiting patiently, we will receive what was promised (Hebrews 6:15).

If I have put my trust in gold or said to pure gold, "you are my security," if I have rejoiced over my great wealth, the fortune my hands had gained, if I have regarded the sun in its radiance or the moon moving in splendor, so that my heart was secretly enticed and my hand offered them a kiss of homage, then these

also would be sins to be judged, for I would have been unfaithful to God on high. (Job 31:24–28)

Read Hebrews 6:13–19

May 7

Be a Blessing for Someone

How often have you told someone you would pray for him or her, but as time goes by, you realize you didn't follow through? Always be firm in your commitment to pray. At times, it seems best to pray together right on the spot, whether you are together in person or on the phone. Intercession is petitioning on behalf of another. It's when you are in touch with God, asking him to lighten another's burden. Your prayer will be a blessing when he or she is renewed with the hope and power of the Holy Spirit. Don't take the influence of the Holy Spirit lightly. He is all-powerful and ready upon your asking.

> May the God of hope fill you with all joy and peace as you trust in him, so that you may overflow with hope by the power of the Holy Spirit. (Romans 15:13)

May 8

Jesus Fellowshipped with Sinners

The only one who was never affected negatively by bad company was Jesus. He is our example of fellowshipping with non-believers, but unless we put him in our pocket when we do, we should beware. In Matthew 9:12, Jesus said, "It is not the healthy who need a doctor, but the sick." He was referring to sinners. When we find ourselves in this situation, we should pray immediately within ourselves and ask God to let his light shine through us and to give us his discernment. I spend time occasionally with non-Christian friends and ask God ahead of time to open a door for me to speak of him and to use me as a vessel for his glory. Sometimes he uses me, and sometimes he actually shows up.

On hearing this, Jesus said, "It is not the healthy who need a doctor, but the sick. (Matthew 9:12)

May 9

There Is No Greater Joy than Your Children Walking in the Truth

I grew up thinking that Catholicism was the one true faith. Mine was a traditional belief, with allegiance to a religion rather than to God himself. As I matured, I was introduced to the idea that it was possible to have a personal relationship with God through Jesus. The scripture presented to me was "Know the truth and the truth shall set you free" (John 8:32). I set out to find the truth, and along the way, I met Jesus. John 14:6 says, "I am the way, the truth, and the life. No one comes to the Father except through me." I found him in a Bible-preaching, nondenominational church. I thought my dad would be proud of me, but he convinced himself that I had abandoned a long, family-held tradition and that the Catholic Church would have all the answers for me. But I found my answers and truth through a personal relationship with God, and to this day, I have great joy in saying that my children walk in this truth and that they are free. There's no greater joy!

> I have no greater joy than to hear that my children are walking in the truth. (3 John 4)

May 10

I have learned to love the darkness of sorrow; there you see the brightness of His face.
—Mrs. Charles E. Cowman, *Streams in the Desert*

Scripture tells us in Genesis that while Joseph was in prison, the Lord was with him, showed him kindness, and granted him favor. God was Joseph's

light amidst an extremely dark and sorrowful time in his life. Joseph seems to have known that God had a plan. There will be times of darkness; no one is exempt. Joseph could have had a great pity party, but he did not sulk and grow discouraged or rebellious. As long as we continue to focus on God, we will continue to see the light. Joseph had great faith and never wavered, even in his deep sorrow over his family disowning him. Joseph's faith set his soul free to hope, and he saw the light that led him to where God wanted him to be. It's a great story. I hope you will read it.

> Joseph's master took him and put him in prison, the place where the king's prisoners were confined. But while Joseph was there in the prison, the Lord was with him; he showed him kindness and granted him favor in the eyes of the prison warden. So the warden put Joseph in charge of all those held in the prison, and he was made responsible for all that was done there. The warden paid no attention to anything under Joseph's care, because the Lord was with Joseph and gave him success in whatever he did. (Genesis 39:20–23)

May 11

Be a Blessing to a Friend

I consider each of my closest friends as a gift from God. To me, a friend is someone who knows all your faults and loves you regardless. That love can only come and last through knowing Jesus. The greatest blessing you can give a friend is prayer, and the one found in Numbers 6:24–26 is a perfect one: "The Lord bless you and keep you; the Lord make his face shine upon you and be gracious to you; the Lord turn his face toward you and give you peace." Likewise, the prayer in Romans 15:13: "May the God of hope fill you with all joy and peace as you trust in Him." Be the kind of friend you want your friends to be to you. You have the same basic need: the love only Jesus can provide.

> I have too much to write to you but I do not want to do so with pen and ink. I hope to see you soon, and we will talk face to face. (3 John 13–14)

> A friend loves at all times. (Proverbs 17:17)

May 12

Is He Enough for Me?

This is a great and awesome question to ask yourself. It brings your relationship with God to a whole new level, doesn't it? For me, it's sometimes yes, sometimes not so sure. I get confused with his ways. Maybe it's because I wonder if I'm enough for him. His word constantly bears witness to the fact that we both are exactly what each other needs. If I can read it and get it into my brain, I should be able to move it from my brain to my heart and into my very soul. The Holy Spirit will make that happen when I stay focused on Jesus and not on myself. Let God influence your heart. Enjoy him and let him enjoy you. It's soul food! In John 17:20–26, read the prayer Jesus prayed for you to his Father. I think you'll find you are enough for him.

> My grace is sufficient for you, for my power is made perfect in weakness. (2 Corinthians 12:9)

May 13

Sex Outside of Marriage

The New Testament abounds with many life circumstances and speaks about God's concept of marriage. These scriptures refer to marriage as between one man and one woman. Sex is a gift to us from God and is for our pleasure and procreation. Sex results in a deep bond between a man and a woman who have committed to spending the rest of their lives together. Surveys show that women who have sex outside of marriage can be negatively affected both mentally and emotionally. I always tell young girls to say no regarding sex before marriage because when that man decides to marry, he will desire a woman who has kept herself pure, the definition of which is innocent, unpolluted, chaste, fresh, and unspoiled. Don't let him spoil you for the one God has chosen for you.

> Marriage should be honored by all, and the marriage bed kept pure, for God will judge the adulterer and all the sexually immoral. (Hebrews 13:4)

May 14

Our Troubles on Earth Are
Worth the Glory in the End

One of my devotional books relays the story of a man blind from birth and later in life having a successful surgery that allowed him his sight. On his wedding day the bandages were removed, and for the first time, he saw his bride face to face. The story relates to our trials on earth and how they don't compare to the glory when we finally see Jesus face to face. The end justifies the means! My philosophy most of my life has been "Things could always be worse." There's always someone else who doesn't have it as good as you, no matter how bad you have it. Count your blessings, and have faith in Jesus' promise that he will return for you. To God be the glory!

> I consider that our present sufferings are not worth comparing with the glory that will be revealed in us. (Romans 8:18)

> Therefore we do not lose heart. Though outwardly we are wasting away, yet inwardly we are being renewed day by day. For our light and momentary troubles are achieving for us an eternal glory that far outweighs them all. So we fix our eyes not on what is seen, but on what is unseen. For what is seen is temporary, but what is unseen is eternal. (2 Corinthians 4:16–18)

May 15

Love One Another with a Pure Heart

Jesus gave so many examples of how to love. If you know him, you know that his love is the purest form of love. True love always comes from a pure heart. First Corinthians 13 is all about love. Verse 2 says that without love we are nothing. Then it goes on to say what love is and what it is not. Love is patient, love is kind. It does not envy, it is not proud. It is not rude or self-seeking, it is not easily angered, and it keeps no record of wrongs. Love does not delight in evil but rejoices with the truth. It always protects, always trusts, always hopes, and always perseveres. (1 Corinthians 13:4–7). The next verse says, "Love never fails" (v. 8). That sounds like a lot of

pressure. I certainly fall short of this every day. But each new morning is an opportunity to ask God to fill us with his kind of love. If we love Jesus with a pure heart, that love will spill from our cup onto the saucer and fill someone else's cup. So what are you waiting for? Drink up!

Now that you have purified yourselves by obeying the truth so that you have sincere love for your brothers, love one another deeply, from the heart. (1 Peter 1:22)

May 16

Pray for One Another's Faith

That's a tall order, especially when our own faith seems to waver at times. In Luke 22, Jesus tells Simon that Satan has asked to sift Simon as wheat. Jesus prays for Simon's faith to not waver. When you feel led to pray for someone but are unsure about what, just ask for his or her faith to be strengthened and God will do the rest. Since the Bible instructs us to pray for one another, we must be obedient. Your obedience will bring a blessing to you both.

Simon, Simon, Satan has asked to sift you as wheat. But I have prayed for you, Simon that your faith may not fail. And when you have turned back, strengthen your brothers. (Luke 22:31–32)

A cord of three strands is not easily broken. (Ecclesiastes 4:12)

May 17

Be Content in All Situations

In the below scriptures Paul is writing to those living in Philippi who loved Jesus. These verses are about adapting to circumstances, good or bad. Because Paul had learned to be content in whatever circumstances, he encouraged the people to do everything through Christ who would strengthen them. I have found that after encouraging others to look to Jesus for peace during trials that I, too, am encouraged. In a daily

devotional, Day by Day, by Billy Graham, he tells the story of a guest at an inn. The owner of the inn says to his guest, "Let me know if there is anything you need and I will show you how to do without it." Stay focused on Jesus and your every need will be met.

> I am not saying this because I am in need, for I have learned to be content whatever the circumstances. I know what it is to be in need, and I know what it is to have plenty. I have learned the secret of being content in any and every situation, whether well fed or hungry, whether living in plenty or in want. I can do everything through him who gives me strength. (Philippians 4:11–13)

May 18

Suffering

God allows suffering to show us his all-sufficient strength and grace. Suffering can make us more conscious of our dependence on him, and often there is no other way to learn faith except through trial. Be still during your times of trouble. Listen intently, and be alert to Satan's schemes to pull you away from God. God will lift you up in due time and restore you. You can't do it on your own. Stay humble, and call on him when you go through tough times. God can change things for you. What a pity it would be to walk through tough times and not come out the other side a changed person for the better.

> Humble yourselves, therefore, under God's mighty hand, that he may lift you up in due time. Cast all your anxiety on him because he cares for you. Be self-controlled and alert. Your enemy the devil prowls around like a roaring lion looking for someone to devour. Resist him, standing firm in the faith, because you know that your brothers throughout the world are undergoing the same kind of sufferings. And the God of all grace, who called you to his eternal glory in Christ, after you have suffered a little while, will himself restore you and make you strong, firm and steadfast. To him be the power for ever and ever. (1 Peter 5:6–11)

May 19

The Cross Always Points to Heaven

In most churches I've been in, the cross is bare. Jesus' body is not portrayed. You are left to paint your own picture of Jesus, a loving redeemer who died for you, was buried, and rose on the third day—all because he loves you. He would have gone to the cross even if you were the only one on earth. And because he rose and went to heaven, you will follow in his steps. He left that bare cross in your view to remind you that he is gone but coming back to get you. Be ready!

> In my Father's house are many rooms; if it were not so, I would have told you. I am going there to prepare a place for you. And if I go ad prepare a place for you, I will come back and take you to be with me that you also may be where I am. You know the way to the place where I am going. (John 14:2–3)

May 20

When We Lose What We Desire, We Acquire What God Wants Us to Have

"What good will it be for a man if he gains the whole world yet forfeits his own soul?" (Matthew 16:26). We must not compromise our faith. Since God is the one who created us, it only makes sense that he knows what we need. Our desires are not always his desires. The Bible gives us guidelines through the Ten Commandments. God didn't expect us to be able to honor them without his help, however. He wanted us to become dependent on him. Be amazed at who he is and what he has done for you. Then open your eyes and see what he wants to give you.

> But seek first his kingdom and his righteousness and all these things will be given to you as well. (Matthew 6:33)

May 21

The Meek Shall Inherit the Earth

Meekness was one of the beatitudes Jesus spoke of in the Sermon on the Mount. His life certainly taught us what meekness and gentleness look like. He says the meek will inherit the earth. That means that because the humble are secure, they are strong, and they have nothing to prove. They don't have to flaunt their strength or use it to rule over others. They are satisfied. Humility leads to meekness; it is strength under control. All this is simply a way of saying that the humble are in touch with reality. This is a spiritual inheritance that comes through a promise made to Abraham and his seed (all those who love Jesus). The spiritual inheritance, of course, is heaven. The promise comes by faith.

> For they shall inherit the earth. (Matthew 5:5)

> Heirs of God. (Matthew 8:17)

> It was not through law that Abraham and his offspring received the promise that he would be heir of the world, but through the righteousness that comes by faith. (Romans 4:13)

> If you belong to Christ, then you are Abraham's seed, and heirs according to the promise. (Galatians 3:29)

May 22

Such a Tiny Offering Compared to Calvary

Do these words flash through your mind when you are patting yourself on the back for doing something great for the Lord? I hope I'm not the only one! The debt that Jesus paid to free us from our chains was with his own blood, and it was the ultimate sacrifice. We can never repay this, no matter if we try a lifetime. And that's just the point: God's gift of salvation is free. That's the way he set it up. No IOUs, no payment plan, no blood; just acceptance of the gift so he alone would be glorified. What do you think God saw in us that was worth his looking our way?

For it is by grace you have been saved, through faith—and this not from yourselves, it is the gift of God—not by works, so that no one can boast. (Ephesians 2:8)

May 23

Grandparents live on the Edge of a Child's Life
Hemming It with Love and Prayers

If you're a grandparent you can probably relate to the above, which I saw on a car window. What a blessing to watch your own children produce a little person who mesmerizes you. At the very beginning, we count their little fingers and toes just as we did with our own child. We watch them grow and give them more love than we knew we had left. We pray and ask the Lord to keep them in a divine bubble with his hand directing it away from the world's temptations. We are gifts to one another—just one more blessing from God's generous plan. You think you can't love them more than you do today ... and then tomorrow comes.

Children's children are a crown to the aged, and parents are the pride of their children. (Proverbs 17:6)

May 24

Speak Up about What Jesus Has Done for You

It's the Great Commission; we are to share our story with others. This is the most effective way to help others accept Jesus into their lives. Your story will be a faith builder. You don't have to memorize scripture in order to tell others. Whatever happened to you doesn't need to be sugar coated; if you're trying to impress, God's power will not be as effective. You are responsible for planting the seed and the Holy Spirit will do the watering. We are only responsible to speak up. Just as the song, This Little Light of Mine says, "This little light of mine, I'm gonna let it shine." You don't

have to be persuasive. It's the sheer unaided power of God because of Jesus. Jesus + 0 = Salvation.

> My prayer is not for them alone. I pray also for those who will believe [in the future] in me through their message. (John 17:20)

May 25

Not Because of Who You Are but Because of *Whose* You Are

We belong to Christ. It's really all about him and nothing about us. When we remember that, we fade out and God fades in, and the "renewed in Christ" person shows up.

God is looking for those whose hearts will always be set on him. Someone who is willing to be nothing so Christ may be all. Someone who will walk in the truth. Let him hold your hand and show you the way. I like to remember whose I am when I'm out in the world dealing with unkind people. It's so tempting to bite back, but Jesus tells us to turn the other cheek (Matthew 5:39). If we stay focused on Jesus, we will be able to act and respond according to Jesus' teachings. And when we lay our head on our pillow at the end of the day it will be ever softer.

> If the Lord delights in a man's way, he makes his steps firm; though he stumble, he will not fall, for the Lord upholds him with his hand. (Proverbs 37:23–24)

May 26

Tithing, Taxes, Bills, Savings, and Lifestyle

God says in Malachi 3:7–10 that when we put our lifestyle before him, we are robbing him. The Old Testament says that tithing is 10 percent of our income, but I have learned over the years that our giving should be from our heart. If God has blessed you financially, perhaps you can give even

more than 10 percent! If we give to God first and then pay our taxes, the rest is ours to spend appropriately on our lifestyle. God says he will bless us for our giving, and that we should actually test him in this. He says he will throw open the floodgates of heaven and pour out an overabundance of blessings. It seems worth a try, doesn't it? Hold God to his promises. I dare you!!

> "Will a man rob God? Yet you rob me. "But you ask, 'How do we rob you?' "In tithes and offerings. You are under a curse - the whole nation of you - because you are robbing me. Bring the whole tithe into the storehouse, that there may be food in my house. Test me in this," says the Lord Almighty, "and see if I will not throw open the floodgates of heaven and pour out so much blessing that you will not have room enough for it." (Malachi 3:8–10)

> Give to Caesar the things that are Caesar's and to God what is God's. (Matthew 22:21)

May 27

The Incarnation:
When God Became Human and
the Eternal Son Became Flesh

Jesus was entirely human when he was on earth—but with God's power. He understands all human emotions and physical pain. He was tempted, required food and sleep, and wept (in John 11:35). When you are down, don't you sometimes need your closest friends to talk to, mainly because they know you so well and can most likely relate? You can trust them to give you the best support and be free of judgment. This is why Jesus' humanness makes him the one we should go to first. Because he's been through it all, he can relate; it's a "been there done that" sort of thing. Let Jesus be your best friend. He will be there for you every time.

> Surely it is not angels he helps, but Abrahams' descendants. For this reason he had to be made like his brothers in every way, in order that he might become a merciful and faithful high priest in

service to God, and that he might make atonement for the sins of the people. Because he himself suffered when he was tempted, he is able to help those who are being tempted. (Hebrews 2:16–18)

May 28

Sanctification:
The Process of Being Made Holy,
Set Apart from the World

Do you see yourself as set apart from the world? Or do you just kind of blend in? If you were on trial for being a Christian, do you think there would be enough evidence to convict you? Read the definition of *sanctification* again. It has two specific parts: being made holy and set apart. We are made holy by God as he disciplines us day by day. We can't make ourselves holy. It is only by enduring hardship through his discipline that we can hope to get there. This is your spiritual act of worship.

> God's divine power has given us everything we need for life and godliness and through that power and his many promises, we can escape the corruption in the world caused by evil desires. The word of God is at work in those who believe. (2 Peter 1:3–4)

May 29

The Transfiguration:
Jesus Praying on the Sacred Mountain
and Visibly Glorified by God

The Transfiguration occurred while Jesus was praying (Luke 9:29). The apostle Peter attested to its historical reality in 2 Peter 1:16–18. Jesus was visibly glorified in the presence of three of his closest disciples, Peter, John, and James. This was an actual physical change in the body of Jesus. The fashion of his countenance was altered (Luke 9:29), his face shone like the sun (Matthew 17:2), and his garments became glistening and exceedingly white (Mark 9:3). Peter, James, and John heard God's voice streaming

down from heaven with honor and glory, saying, "This is my Son whom I have chosen; listen to him" (Matthew 9:7).

May 30

The Lord, Our Divine Teacher

Everything you've always wanted to know about life is given to us in God's holy word, the Bible. God is our divine teacher. Many authors of the Bible stories spoke directly to Jesus and heard his parables about life. He was the greatest of all teachers. He spent almost thirty years from the time he was twelve preaching in the temples and out by the rivers in the countryside until his death at thirty-three. He taught us about his will and how to pray and obey. He told us to pass these teachings onto our children. Are you doing that?

> Only be careful, and watch yourselves closely so that you do not forget the things your eyes have seen or let them slip from your heart as long as you live. Teach them to your children and to their children after them. (Deuteronomy 4:9)

> Teach me to do your will, for you are my God; may your good Spirit lead me on level ground. (Psalm 143:10)

May 31

Wine and Beer, Money and Pride

Anything can be evil depending on our use of it. Wine, beer, money, success, honors, and other such things, are not to be had in excess. The Bible says, "Do not linger over wine" (Proverbs 23:30). A side note says "drunkenness." Anything in excess that takes us away from the Lord is not in his plan. Too much of anything can affect our judgment because our minds are diverted from Jesus. You can become arrogant and unwise, making you forget "whose you are." Always consider your motivation and do not be lead astray.

The love of money is the root of all evil; it makes people wander from the truth. (1 Timothy 6:10)

Pride goes before destruction. (Proverbs 16:18)

June 1

The Seed of Integrity

We reap what we sow, right? Usually … but not always. We can do our best to "train a child in the way he should go" (Proverbs 22:6), but our children still have free will and may wander for a time. When they are young adults, it's time to let go. Now it is between them and God. When they are older and out in the world making decisions, your actions and words will make them see how much God has influenced your life and they will seek it. It must be their decision, though. They will have learned that the standards of the world are difficult to keep up with and are different from God's. Remember, when Adam and Eve were in the garden, they had a perfect parent and they still rebelled.

> The righteous man leads a blameless life; blessed are his children after him. (Proverbs 20:7)

June 2

The Folded Napkin

The Bible tells us about the empty tomb after Jesus rose from the dead. It says that the napkin, which was placed over the face of Jesus when he was buried, was found neatly folded and placed at the head of the stony tomb, not just tossed aside with the other grave clothes. Was that significant? Let me help you decide. As a Hebrew tradition in that day, a young Jewish servant would serve his master by setting a perfect table for dinner. The servant would watch at a distance to take note when the master was finished eating so he could promptly remove the dinnerware. If the master was finished, he would rise from the table and toss his napkin onto the plate. But if the master rose from the table and folded his napkin neatly

and laid it beside his plate, the servant understood that it meant "I'm not finished yet. I'm coming back." So...... I guess it is significant!

> The burial cloth that had been around Jesus' head was folded up by itself, separate from the linen. (John 20:7)

Read John 20:1-8

June 3

We Conquer Persecution When We Act Like Christ

Jesus is definitely our best example of conquering persecution. I know it's hard to follow in his footsteps, but we are told over and over again that it is possible. Many of the things he did on earth he did as an example for us. So if he can turn his cheek to his persecutors, we can do so with his help. Forgiveness and love are difficult to hand out freely to those we don't feel deserve it. Remember, because Jesus was persecuted we will also be persecuted. The people hated Jesus without reason. Don't try to lead a godly life on your own. Accept Jesus' help, and then you can give him the glory for the results. That's what it is all about, right?

> Everyone who wants to live a godly life in Christ Jesus will be persecuted. (2 Timothy 3:12)

> Remember the words I spoke to you: 'No servant is greater than his master.' If they persecuted me, they will persecute you also. If they obeyed my teaching, they will obey yours also. (John 15:20)

June 4

God Is in Control of the Outcome, Not the Process

God gives us free will. Sometimes I find having my own free will rather frightening. If God is in control of the outcome but I am in control of

the process, that means I could get pretty beat up along the way, right? Accepting Jesus into our lives and allowing him to be the Lord of our lives lowers the hurdles and softens the fall. We will still be in the race, but because he is in control of the outcome, we win. Being on his team is a win-win situation. The only part of my free will I'm content with is when I freely accept God's Son, Jesus, into my life.

Read Romans 8.

June 5

Sometimes Others' Illnesses Are Our Trials

We all experience the hardship of a loved one's illness some time in our life, whether it is a child or an adult. If the illness causes death, it can become an even greater burden for us to carry. God does not expect us to carry it alone, however. Psalm 34:18–19 says, "The Lord is close to the broken hearted and saves those who are crushed in spirit—the Lord delivers them from their troubles." God is well aware of your sorrow and may be using you to complete something in the life of a loved one. Occasionally, when trials come, they may not be all about you. A trial of any kind may not have anything to do with sin but may have everything to do with God's love.

> As you know, it was because of an illness that I first preached the gospel to you. Even though my illness was a trial to you, you did not treat me with contempt or scorn. (Galatians 4:13–14)

June 6

When Earth Is Shaken, God Remains

Have you ever watched the perseverance of an ant? I admit I have been entertained many times by their determination. Not only do they carry several times their own weight, but if they get near their destination and fall, they start all over again and persevere until they are where they want to be. When your life, or your year, or your day is shaken beyond your

expectations, remember this promise: God is omniscient and omnipresent. He knows and understands your predicament. Like the ant focusing on his destination, we need to stay focused on Jesus. When he sees you falling back, he will stretch out his hand as a safety net. This is an everlasting covenant between you and God.

> Blessed is the man who perseveres under trial, because when he has stood the test, he will receive the crown of life that God has promised to those who love him. (James 1:12)

June 7

Pray for a Kingdom Experience

When praying seems to hold a mystery, it is difficult to know how to talk to God. When someone is heavy on your heart, and you are totally unclear what to pray for, ask God to give that person a kingdom experience. God already knows anyway. Nothing surprises him. A kingdom experience covers a vast amount of area, so we can be sure God will intervene at the proper time with the best answer—even if it isn't what we had in mind. We were obedient to pray, and now the situation is in his hands. Remember, he has the whole world in his hands! He will do the sculpting.

> And he who searches our hearts knows the mind of the Spirit, because the Spirit intercedes for the saints in accordance with God's will. (Romans 8:27)

June 8

Depend on the Performance of the Promiser

Claiming God's promises has been a part of my daily prayers recently. All throughout the old and new testaments you will find promises of his faithfulness. Waiting for God to answer our prayers is very difficult, but when we do receive a victory, it strengthens our hope in the future. Always remember how God has worked in your past circumstances and

know that everything is done in his timing, not yours. Don't pick your mercies green.

> The Lord is faithful to all his promises. (Psalm 145:13)

Read Leviticus. God will send his rain in its season.

June 9

You Cannot Exhaust the Power of the Holy Spirit

This is great news for us! Just when we think we can't ask for another miracle, the Holy Spirit comes alongside us and whispers, "Make my day!" You can picture God's power filtering through Jesus and then picking up speed as it goes into the Holy Spirit and finally lands deliberately on us. We are to pray without ceasing because it pleases God. Never determine that you have asked too much of him, and keep in mind that we are not praying only for an answer but also because it is how we communicate with God. That's why he created us, to have a relationship with him, and he wants to hear from us daily. Sometimes we don't have what we want because we haven't asked for it.

> As God has said: "I will live with them and walk among them, and I will be their God, and they will be my people." (2 Corinthians 6:16)

> The Lord detests the sacrifice of the wicked, but the prayer of the upright pleases him. (Proverbs 15:8)

June 10

Life Is a Battle; Fight Like a Winner

Nothing worth fighting for is ever easy. All the suffering will be worth the glory at the end. God's word is full of encouragement to keep on keeping

on. It's not always that easy though, right? When you know you'll never get out of your wheelchair, or you come home from war with an arm or leg missing, it's difficult to see the light at the end of the tunnel. God has provided us with his word, counselors, prayer partners, and his promise that he will never leave us or forsake us. God is hovering near you. Use his presence as your weapon. Fight the good fight, and keep your eye on the prize. Hide his word in your heart.

> For the battle is not yours, but God's. Stand firm and see the deliverance the Lord will give you. (2 Chronicles 20:15–17)

> I have fought the good fight, I have finished the race, I have kept the faith. Now there is in store for me the crown of righteousness, which the Lord, the righteous Judge, will award to me on that day—and not only to me, but also to all who have longed for his appearing. (2 Timothy 4:7)

June 11

Sorrowful, Yet Always Rejoicing

When do you call on God the most? When things are going well? Or when life becomes tough? When things are good, it's easy to praise God and give him thanks, sometimes absentmindedly. It may not always seem that we are actually connecting, though. When difficulties come, whether through fear or sorrow, we tend to get on our knees and truly seek the Lord. Godly sorrow always leads to repentance. That's just the way he designed it so we would reach out in prayer to him. Prayer builds a relationship with God. We shouldn't think that we pray to get an answer but to communicate with him. That's one of the reasons he created us. He loves it when we call! And we can delight in each other!

> Yet now I am happy, not because you were made sorry but because your sorrow led you to repentance. (2 Corinthians 7:9)

June 12

It Is Not Enough to Do Right;
We Need to *Be* Right

Some religions believe that in order to get to heaven you are required to do good works, or "do" right. If that were true, why would Jesus have had to die for us? We actually just need to "be" right with God, and that's a lot easier and less tiring. If we are too busy "doing" good in the church or elsewhere, and don't take special, personal time with Jesus, we've missed the boat. God's grace allows us our ticket into heaven. Only through Jesus can we "do" anything "right" anyway! Seek him and the good works will come naturally. Good works are a *symptom* of a Christian, not a cause.

> I do not understand what I do for what I want to do I do not do, but what I hate, I do. I have the desire to do what is good, but I cannot carry it out. (Romans 7:15–18)

> For it is by grace you have been saved, through faith—and this is not from yourselves, it is the gift of God— not by works, so that no one can boast. (Ephesians 2:8–9)

June 13

God's Passion:
The Display of His Glory and
the Delight of Your Heart

Answering our prayers is God's passion. Those answers come not only to give us joy but also to display his glory. It's kind of like when we're happy, God is happy. When we are close to God and living in obedience to him, our desires fall in line with his. His answering our prayers is a form of communication with us. He is delighted to see us living in his will and lets his glory shine through us. We are committed to one another because of Jesus.

Commit your way to the Lord; trust in him and he will do this: He will make your righteousness shine like the dawn, the justice of your cause like the noon day sun. (Psalm 36:5)

But seek first his kingdom and his righteousness, and all these things will be given to you as well. (Matthew 6:33)

June 14

Parents: Reveal the Fatherhood of God to Your Children

Ten ways you can reveal the fatherhood of God to your children:

1. Speak well of the Lord's greatness.
2. Run to him.
3. Obey him.
4. Trust him.
5. Ask him.
6. Turn to him as your source.
7. Let your children hear you bless the Lord in prayer before eating.
8. Let your kids hear your heart, not your brain.
9. Show thankfulness for God's forgiveness.
10. Let your children see that God truly moves you.

From everlasting to everlasting the Lord's love is with those who fear him (reverence) and his goodness is with his children's children—with those who keep his covenant and remember to obey his teachings. (Psalm 103:17–18)

June 15

Closeness to God Is about
Movement, Not Position

Even God can't steer a vehicle that isn't moving. We need to continue opening the doors he puts in front of us. Let him use you as a vessel for his purposes and move in the power of his Holy Spirit. Closeness to God comes by pursuing a relationship with him. God will never be finished with you, so don't ever be satisfied with where you are in him. Keep moving toward God and you will find spiritual rest for your soul.

This is the way, walk in it. (Isaiah 30:21)

Ask where the good way is and walk in it and you will find rest for your souls. (Jeremiah 6:16)

June 16

We Learn Faith by Trial, the
Reason for Our Suffering

When we are suffering it is difficult to depend on ourselves, and when we are down we are more conscious of our dependence on him. Suffering builds our faith because it shows his all-sufficient grace much better than if we were exempt from pressure and trial. Trials actually strengthen our faith and cause us to hang onto that trust that will bring us through it. God never said he would keep us from trials, only that he would go through them with us. Always look back on the times God has been there for you and remember how your faith was strengthened. God allows suffering to achieve his purposes.

Our suffering is worth the glory that is coming. (Romans 8:18)

My grace is sufficient for you. (2 Corinthians 12:9)

June 17

We Pray for Healing; We
Have a Duty to Do So

When Jesus walked on the earth, many people flocked to him for healing. He expects us to pray for healing and tells us that through the Holy Spirit, we will be able to heal just as he did. It takes a lot of faith to pray for healing, whether it's for our self, another person, or our land (2 Chronicles 7:14). After many years of praying for healing, I've learned a new way to pray. Like Jesus in the Lord's Prayer, we must be willing to say, "Not my will, but yours be done" (Matthew 26:39). When we are obedient to pray, we must trust that God is sovereign and all-powerful. We must remember his promises. The outcome will be according to his plan, not ours. The healing may take place on earth or in heaven. Nevertheless, your prayer has been heard.

> Is any one of you sick? He should call the elders of the church to pray over him and anoint him with oil in the name of the Lord. And the prayer offered in faith will make the sick person well; the Lord will raise him up. (James 5:14–16)

> While he was saying this, a synagogue leader came and knelt before him and said, "My daughter has just died. But come and put your hand on her, and she will live." Jesus got up and went with him, and so did his disciples. Just then a woman who had been subject to bleeding for twelve years came up behind him and touched the edge of his cloak. She said to herself, "If I only touch his cloak, I will be healed." Jesus turned and saw her. "Take heart, daughter," he said, "your faith has healed you." And the woman was healed at that moment. (Matthew 9:18-22)

June 18

Six Things God Hates

According to Proverbs 6:16, God hates the following:

1. Pride (conceit and arrogance)
2. Lying (speaking falsely)
3. Manipulation (wicked schemes)
4. Evil activity (immorality)
5. Busybodies (stirring up dissension among brothers and sisters)
6. Hands that shed innocent blood (murder)

Ask him to show you your sin.

June 19

Stay Away from Faultfinding

This is such a tough subject. God says a lot about it in his word. Other terms for faultfinding are *hypocrite*, *condemnation*, and *judging others*. Usually, the fault we find in others ends up being something we dislike in ourselves, so the judgment is actually on us coming indirectly from God. Matthew 7:4 says, "How can you say to your brother, 'Let me take the speck out of your eye,' when all the time there is a plank in your own." God calls these people hypocrites. We should be encouraging others, and through that act of obedience, we will be helping ourselves. God is the only true judge.

> Do not judge, or you too will be judged. For in the same way you judge others, you will be judged, and with the measure you use, it will be measured to you. Why do you look at the speck of sawdust in your brother's eye and pay no attention to the plank in your own eye? You hypocrite, first take the plank out of your own eye, and then you will see clearly to remove the speck from your brother's eye. (Matthew 7:1–5)

June 20

Instruct the Next Generation

This generation and the next will certainly need hope. To lose hope is to lose God. We are the ones to encourage them through the scriptures. Everything that was written in the past was written to teach and help us to endure. We must teach our children at a young age to stand firm in the Lord. He will always show us a way out of tempting situations that could possibly lead to evil actions. The Bible is written for the present and the future generations. Each generation is affected by the prior generation, both good and bad. "All things work for good for those that love the Lord" (Romans 8:28). One person can make a difference. Be a rainbow in someone's cloud. If not now, when?

> Let this be written for a future generation, that a people not yet created may praise the Lord. (Psalm 102:18)

> Fathers, do not exasperate your children; instead, bring them up in the training and instruction of the Lord. (Ephesians 6:4)

June 21

Keep Oil in Your Tank: The Oil of the Holy Spirit

After Jesus rose from the grave on what we call Easter Sunday, he walked with his disciples and told them he had to go away. He also told them, however, that he would not leave them alone but would send the Holy Spirit to guide them. If you have accepted God's gift of Jesus, and have him at the center of your life, you have the Holy Spirit too! It's a package deal: Father, Son, and Holy Spirit. Ask God every morning to fill you with all the fruit of the Holy Spirit: love, joy, peace, patience, kindness, goodness, gentleness, faithfulness, and self- control (Galatians 5:22). You won't get far on an empty tank!

And I will ask the Father, and he will give you another advocate to help you and be with you forever. But the Advocate, the Holy Spirit, whom the Father will send in my name, will teach you all things and will remind you of everything I have said to you. (John 14:16, 26)

June 22

Ignorance Is a Lack of Information

You've probably heard the phrases "Ignorance is bliss" and "What you don't know can't hurt you." Ignorance of the facts doesn't mean reality won't happen. Our minds are capable of storing an enormous amount of information and details, both worldly and spiritually. If a driver doesn't know the bridge is out ahead, it doesn't mean he won't end up in the water. If a person doesn't know there is a hell, it doesn't mean he won't end up there some day. If only they had more information they could have made better choices. Listen to the Holy Spirit. Learn as much as possible about what Jesus has to offer you so you won't have to plead ignorance on judgment day.

> My son, pay attention to what I say; listen closely to my words. Do not let them out of your sight, keep them within your heart; for they are life to those who find them and health to a man's whole body. (Proverbs 4:20–23)

> The discerning heart seeks knowledge, but the mouth of a fool feeds on folly. (Proverbs 15:14)

June 23

A Storm or Trial Does Not Mean
You Are out of God's Will

God allows trials and storms into your life to strengthen you, build your faith, and develop you into what he desires for you. Read about the lives of Paul, Joseph, and many others in the Bible, and you will see they weren't

walking down Easy Street. Their strong faith and obedience helped them to persevere in extremely difficult and almost impossible situations. All through the storm they were in God's will. No trial or sorrow is ever outside the hem of Jesus' robe.

> Blessed is the man who perseveres under trial, because when he has stood the test he will receive the crown of life that God has promised to those who love him. (James 1:12)

June 24

Do Your Good Deeds in Secret

We like to get a pat on the back every once in a while, don't we? Sometimes we are tempted to look good in front of others; that would be our human nature. Giving to the needy, praying, or fasting are just a few examples. It's much more rewarding to give an anonymous gift of money to the church, whether it be large or small. Or how about helping serve food to those less fortunate without letting your family or friends know about it? Just let it be between you and God. He will see what is done in secret and will reward you. It won't come as a blue ribbon or a gold watch but as a sense of his peace, love, joy, or bonding in your relationship with him—all things the world can't give or take away. Ponder the following words of Jesus from the book of Matthew. God is the only one easy to please.

> Be careful not to do your "acts of righteousness" before men, to be seen by them. If you do, you will have no reward from your Father in heaven. (Matthew 6:1–4)

> When you fast, do not look somber as the hypocrites do, for they disfigure their faces to show men they are fasting. I tell you the truth, they have received their reward in full. (Matthew 6:16–18)

June 25

Two Coals Burning Together Stay
Hotter Than One Burning Alone

The Great Commission (or command) is "Go tell the world, tell it on the mountain that Jesus Christ is born" (Matthew 28:16-20). Jesus gave us the command to tell others what he has done for us. In order for us to stay on fire for him, we need to hang out with other Christians. We need to add kindling and fan the flame. We are strong and more powerful in numbers. Jesus didn't appoint just one man to spread the good news. He had twelve disciples who went out two by two to tell the world that Jesus saves. Don't be a hermit Christian!

> Then the eleven disciples went to Galilee, to the mountain where Jesus had told them to go. When they saw him, they worshiped him; but some doubted. Then Jesus came to them and said, "All authority in heaven and on earth has been given to me. Therefore go and make disciples of all nations, baptizing them in the name of the Father and of the Son and of the Holy Spirit, and teaching them to obey everything I have commanded you. And surely I am with you always, to the very end of the age." (Matthew 28:16-20)

June 26

God Disciplines; He doesn't Punish

Why does God allow certain travesties in our lives, over and over again? Perhaps because he has a much broader perspective than we do and sees the road and the outcome. We need to ask God what it is he wants us to learn from our downfalls. We need to understand he is not angry with us, although he may be looking for repentance. Luke 15:10 says, "There is rejoicing in the presence of the angels of God over one sinner who repents." God is not hovering, ready to bring down the hammer on us at our first flirt with sin. He does, however, use circumstances to bridle us when we are outside his will. He is our heavenly Father who disciplines us out of a deep and pure love. Be aware of the leading of his Holy Spirit. It's the first sign he wants to have a conversation with you.

Teach me to do your will for you are my God; may your good spirit lead me on level ground. (Psalm 143:10)

Read (Hebrews 12:4–11)

June 27

Grieve, but Not Without Hope

We have all experienced grief at some point in our lives. Even Jesus experienced grief to the point of sweating blood during his crucifixion. Each of us can give our own description of how it rips the soul in two. It can be a time when we either turn to God or turn away in anger and disappointment. The grief journey doesn't require anyone to walk it alone. Feel confident that God is reaching down to give you all that you need. Be hopeful that his hands will warm and heal your grieving soul.

God is close to the broken hearted. (Psalm 34:18)

He heals the broken hearted and binds up their wounds. (Psalm 147:3)

June 28

Meet God in the Inner Chamber of Your Spirit

Whether you believe in God or not doesn't negate the fact that he exists, always has and always will. He created your soul with an emptiness that can be filled only by knowing him intimately. We can't get filled through our emotions; it must be strictly by faith in him. He has prepared a holy ground for you to walk on. He has taken off his sandals and bids you to do the same. Come, meet him inside in the therapeutic garden.

"Do not come any closer," God said. "Take off your sandals for the place you are standing is holy ground." (Exodus 3:5)

June 29

Don't Settle for a False Normal

What would represent a false normal? Trying to be someone you're not? How about Hollywood? Believing a lie about yourself? Thinking you're not good enough for God? I believe anything that is not of God is a false normal. God is the only absolute. Don't settle for less than what God wants to give you. He has a plan for you that will overshadow any of your desires. Walk on God's path, and do the best with the tools he's given you. Don't let your pride keep you from learning God's truth. His truth will set you free, and that's about as normal as you can get. God helps us depend on him by giving us the Ten Commandments. He knew we wouldn't be able to keep them. Please note they are not called the Ten Suggestions! They are in the Bible for a good reason. It's part of the grace that he has lavished on us (Ephesians 1:8). He loves us with an undying love. Thinking that he doesn't want us to love him in return would be a "false normal."

Know the truth and the truth will set you free. (John 8:32)

June 30

Be Bread for the World

Much of the world we live in is in the state of spiritual starvation and bankruptcy. The fields are ripe, but the workers are few. We, the believers, are the workers. We need to take our knowledge of God and his gift of Jesus and feed the starving and weary world. We need to pass on our stories and share our blessings. We are God's messengers. We are to carry the light for others to see the way. Jesus is the way. He said he was.

Jesus declared, "I am the bread of life." (John 6:35)

Then he said to his disciples, "The harvest is plentiful but the workers are few. Ask the Lord of the harvest, therefore, to send out workers into his harvest field." (Matthew 9:37)

July 1

Come as You Are and
Bring What You Have to God

I have several friends and loved ones who do not attend church. My invitation to them is either ignored or they pacify me with, "sure, maybe someday." It's difficult to understand why they wouldn't want to take advantage of everything God has to offer. Maybe they think they have to change their ways first so as to present something better to God. I believe they have it backward. First you bring what you have to God and *he* will make the changes. It's so much easier that way. Jesus died to make us presentable to God. If you don't believe that, wasn't he crucified in vain? Come as you are. God will be waiting.

> If we confess our sins he is faithful and just and will forgive us our sins and purify us from all unrighteousness. (1 John 1:9)

July 2

Am I Blind or Is the World Just Dark?

I believe there is good in the world. The good represents God's light. It seems dim right now, doesn't it? You don't need 20/20 vision to see that the world has grown darker over time. I'm talking about a spiritual darkness. Darkness represents evil or, if you want to put a name on it, Satan. God instructs us to stay walking in the light because that is where he is. Be more perceptive of the things of God and less tempted by the things of the world. What God gives us is permanent; what the world gives will surely decay.

> Your word is a lamp unto my feet and a light for my path. (Psalm 119:105)

> Everything is permissible—but not everything is beneficial. (1 Corinthians 10:23)

July 3

Has anyone ever seen God's Face?

God has shown his glory many times, but he only shows the effect of himself, as in the burning bush with Moses or as a bright light with Jacob. God said in Exodus that no man could see his face and live. I think the lyrics of the song "Imagine" express what it might be like when we get to heaven.

> Surrounded by your glory what will my heart feel?
> Will I dance for you, Jesus, or in awe of you be still?
> Will I stand in your presence or to my knees will I fall?
> Will I sing Hallelujah? Will I be able to speak at all?
> I can only imagine.

I'm not even sure we will see God's face when we are in heaven. Maybe it will still just be a great light and the power of his presence. The book of Revelation says we will see Jesus, as he will be doing the separating of the good from the bad and judging the bad. Only those whose names are written in the Lamb's Book of Life will enter into life everlasting with him. Is your name in the book?

> No one has ever seen God, but God the One and only, who is at the Father's side, has made him known. (John 1:18)

July 4

People Who Know Jesus
Don't Live in Darkness

Darkness refers to sin. If we profess to know Jesus but go on continually sinning, we may not be aware of the whole truth. We may be walking in darkness. Once we put Christ in the center of our lives, his desires become our desires. Our demeanor changes, and we are drawn into a process that slowly refines us. We have the Holy Spirit to help us stay away from temptation; we won't have to do it alone. Jesus will change our lives, and

we will want to share what he has done for us with others. Now that we are walking in the light, the darkness is much more apparent. Once Jesus touches us, we see everything in a new light. Look for the light; it's in God's word.

Once I was blind, but now I see. (John 9:25)

Your word is a lamp unto my feet. (Psalm 119:105)

July 5

Gossip Betrays a Confidence

Even if the entire town knows about it, and even if it is true, if you heard something in confidence, you need to keep it in your own heart and not stir up others' hearts with it. It all happens so quickly. Even a forest fire starts with a small spark (James 3:5). You can change the whole course of a person's life with gossip. Woe be to you. When you feel that tug of the Holy Spirit to question your motives, listen up.

May the words of my mouth and the meditation of my heart be pleasing in your sight my Lord and redeemer. (Psalm 19:14)

A perverse man stirs up dissension, and a gossip separates close friends. (Proverbs 16:28)

July 6

God Isn't Finished With You Yet

No matter where you are in your life, you can be sure that God is working something out. No matter how many times you fall, he's right there with his healing balm and his hand out to give you what you need. He's a very patient God and never gives up on you. He has a very specific plan for you and will make it clear as you seek him. You are one of God's chosen people and have a stake in his kingdom. Don't ever forget whose you are.

He who began a good work in you will be faithful to complete it. (Philippians 1:6)

July 7

Christianity Is a Team Sport; Don't Go It Alone

If Christianity were a sport, would you tryout? Would you play? What would some of the rules be, and what would be the goal of the game? Would there be boundaries and penalties? How would we pick our teammates, and what qualifications would be required? Seriously, we know that Christianity isn't a game. Its reality comes through the death of Jesus. There are no qualifications, and anyone can sign up. All believers come together for the purpose of praying and breaking bread together and lifting one another up. God calls us the body of Christ. He arranges the parts in the body, every one of them, just as he wants them to be (1 Corinthians 12:18). He never meant for anyone to act alone. Be part of the team, God's team.

> All the believers were together and had everything in common. They sold property and possessions to give to anyone who had need. Every day they continued to meet together in the temple courts. They broke bread in their homes and ate together with glad and sincere hearts. (Acts 2:44–46)

> For just as each of us has one body with many members, and these members do not all have the same function, so in Christ we, though many, form one body, and each member belongs to all the others. We have different gifts, according to the grace given to each of us. If your gift is prophesying, then prophesy in accordance with your faith; if it is serving, then serve; if it is teaching, then teach; if it is to encourage, then give encouragement; if it is giving, then give generously; if it is to lead, do it diligently; if it is to show mercy, do it cheerfully. (Romans 12:4–8)

July 8

Difficulties Change the Way We Deal with God and Others

God can bring good out of any difficult situation. However, we do need to remember that it is in his timing, not ours (2 Peter 3:8). Don't pluck your mercy green; wait for it to ripen. Whether it is dealing with a spiritual problem or your neighbor or friend, seek God's wisdom. He wants us to learn something from it. How meaningless would it be to go through something tragic and not come through it a better person? Ask God what he wants you to get out of your trials, and he will be faithful to show you. Then remember to praise him for the difficulty. Closer, stronger, healthier relationships and a better way of life are worth the perseverance.

> We also rejoice in our sufferings, because we know that suffering produces perseverance; perseverance, character; and character, hope. (Romans 5:3–4)

July 9

Don't Fall Prey to False Teachings

Scoffers post on the Web, "Jesus isn't coming back." But Jesus says in John 14:2–3 that he *is* preparing a place for us and *will* come back and take us there. Second Peter 3:8–9 says, "The Lord is not slow in keeping his promises he is patient, not wanting anyone to perish." Always seek God for your answers. He is truth and the only absolute. He has made many promises and cannot break them. Cling to those promises as if your life depended on it—because it does!

> For the time will come when men will not put up with sound doctrine. Instead, to suit their own desires, they will gather around them a great number of teachers to say what their itching ears want to hear. They will turn their ears away from the truth and turn aside to myths. (2 Timothy 4:3–4)

Know the truth and the truth will set you free. (John 8:32)

July 10

Tough Times Don't Last,
but God's People Do

During tough times be humble and pray and fast. Fasting increases prayer time, praising releases fear, and reading reminds us of God's promises. Matthew 6:16–18 says *when* we fast, not *if* we fast. Tough times come and go, like the seasons. Each time they come, we need to look back and see how God was there for us and how he helped us through it. He never takes us around the trouble but rather through it so we can learn and grow from the experience. Think of a negative situation as a positive opportunity to make life better.

> If my people, who are called by my name, will humble themselves and pray and seek my face and turn from their wicked ways, then will I hear from heaven and will forgive their sin and will heal their land. (2 Chronicles 7:14)

July 11

God Uses Regular People
to Minister for Him

God gives us several examples in the Bible of how he brings people through calamity. Following are just a few:

Abraham—Genesis 11:31–25:10 (the journeys of Abraham)
Moses—Exodus, Deuteronomy
Noah—Genesis
Saul—1 Samuel
David—1 and 2 Samuel
Solomon—2 Chronicles
Peter and Paul—the New Testament Gospels and the book of Acts

Jonah
Mary (the mother of Jesus)—Matthew and Luke
Esther
Daniel
Joseph—Genesis
Nehemiah
Joshua
Elizabeth—Luke 1:5–58

The list goes on and on and guess who it includes? You! God doesn't look for people who are able, he looks for people who are available. Read about some of them and be inspired.

July 12

Are You in the Church Where God Can Use You Best?

What do you look for in a church? I have known people who have taken years to find the "right fit." Some like the sermons, but the music is too loud. Some like the music but don't feel the ministries are run correctly. Yet others complain because communion is served too often or not often enough. I believe God will show you where he wants you planted if you will seek him about it. He will also transplant you after a period of time if he thinks you will bloom better somewhere else. Have you ever visited a dead church? If you don't feel the movement of the Holy Spirit, move on. Look for children, youth, and adult ministries. Look for a church that is reaching out to the community and has Bible-based messages. Does the worship time and music ministry allow you to get into the presence of God? Do the messages give a down-to-earth, balanced portrayal of God the Father, Son, and Holy Spirit? Seeking these things will help you end up where God can use you best. Remember, it's not all about you receiving what you need but also about you giving to others and encouraging them. Don't think God can't use you in church. Be open to his calling.

Those who seek the Lord lack no good thing. (Psalm 34:10)

But encourage each other daily so that none of you may be hardened by sin's deceitfulness. (1 Timothy 4:18)

July 13

God's Power Lies in Earthen Vessels

Each and every one of us is a vessel to be used by God. He gives us the wisdom and strength required to carry out his commands. You will find that being used by God for his purpose is a humbling and powerful experience. We are usually not even aware that he is using us. Let God shape and mold you until you become like a fine perfume, and then let him pour out the fragrance on those in need. Always seek the leading of the Holy Spirit in your actions and words. But never seek the glory but rather give it all to God. Remember, it's not about whether you are able to accomplish what he asks of you, for with him all things are possible. (Matthew 19:26)

> You will receive power when the Holy Spirit comes on you; and you will be my witnesses in Jerusalem, and in all Judea and Samaria, and to the ends of the earth. (Acts 1:8)

July 14

We Are Slaves to Anything That Masters Us

What are you a slave to? What or who is your idol? What takes you away from your time with God? A God-centered life is the only way to stay focused on Jesus. Examples of an idol are alcohol, work, gambling, movies, videos, shopping, money, exercising, sports, hobbies, possessions, etc. None of these things is evil, but if any have a hold on you, it could lead to trouble. Only you can release yourself from a bondage that fills too much of your time. Seek God and his kingdom first and these things will be given to you as well (Luke 12:31).

> Where your treasure is there your heart is also. (Matthew 6:21)

> A man is a slave to whatever has mastered him. (2 Peter 2:19)

July 15

What Is the Real Issue?

Do you think we should have issues with the Lord? Do you ever wonder if you have one and what it might be? It's okay to wonder and be inquisitive; however, if there is an issue so strong that it blinds you to the leading of the Holy Spirit, you need to deal with that promptly. You can ask God if there is an issue between the two of you, but don't ask if you're not ready to listen and make a change. God's word says he will always be available to you. Realizing what the real issue is will open new doors for you, and you will enter into the restful life of Christ's fullness.

Read John 4:4–26 about the Samaritan woman by the well. Jesus brings up her husband, the real issue, which was about her sin.

July 16

Other People's Choices Affect Us

Sometimes this affect is positive, other times negative. Many people, even Christians, make bad choices without realizing the ripple effect. Sometimes it is our choice, whether it affects us or not, such as infidelity, breaking a promise, careless living, inconsideration, being unkind, gossiping, striving too hard for success … the list goes on and on. Have you made any choices that have negatively affected your relationships? Ask God to show you what I'm talking about and if you need to ask for forgiveness. It will be like mending an old sweater, making it useful again.

> I have chosen the way of truth; I have set my heart on your laws.
> (Psalm 119:30)

July 17

"Humility Comes Before Honor"
(Proverbs 15:33)

Jesus was the most humble man to walk the face of the earth. His humility certainly is a great example of how to put others first. When others treated him badly or were accusatory, he asked his Father in heaven to forgive them. He didn't worry about his self-worth. Jesus knew his purpose and worked toward it, not allowing others to defeat him. As Proverbs 15:33 says, "Humility comes before honor," and Jesus humbly and obediently carried his cross to a death that exalted him in the end. Clothe yourself in humility, stay focused on Jesus, and work toward God's purpose without hesitation.

> Young men, in the same way be submissive to those who are older. All of you, clothe yourselves with humility toward one another, because, "God opposes the proud but gives grace to the humble." (1 Peter 5:5)

July 18

What Must Go from Your Life to Make
Room for What God Has for You?

Simon was full of bitterness and captive to sin. The Samaritan woman was living in sin, as she was not married to the man she lived with. I once heard a story about a man who dreamed that he was having a tour of heaven. He came to a room filled with beautiful packages with large satin bows. When he asked about them, he was told the boxes contained all the blessings God couldn't give him because his life was too cluttered with sin and worldly things. He had spent too much time on his own desires rather than seeking God's desire for his life. If you ever wonder what you need to get rid of, just ask God; he'll tell you straight up. I hope when I get to heaven there are no beautiful packages with my name on them. The only place I want my name is in the Lamb's Book of Life.

> Do not love the world or anything in the world. If anyone loves the world, the love of the Father is not in him. For everything in

the world—the cravings of sinful man, the lust of his eyes and the boasting of what he has and does—comes not from the Father but from the world. The world and its desires pass away but the man who does the will of God lives forever. (1 John 2:15)

Read Acts 8:4–23.

July 19

Satan Enjoys Bringing Us Down When We Least Expect It

Satan likes to get us on the wide path that leads to destruction. We need to read God's word and do what it says; otherwise we deceive ourselves. We need to be ready for whatever comes our way. Reading and knowing the Bible is the best way to get close to God and understand his will. When the tsunami hit Japan in 2011, entire towns were destroyed and nearly fifty thousand people died or were missing or injured. It actually shifted earth on its axis. This all came as a total surprise to the natives and those vacationing there. This is how Satan works; he sneaks up on us when we're unaware. We think we've got the world by the tail, and in a flash, it's turned upside down. Beware!

> Be self-controlled and alert. Your enemy the devil prowls around like a roaring lion looking for someone to devour. (1 Peter 5:9)

> Do not merely listen to the word and so deceive yourselves. Do what it says. (James 1:22)

July 20

Who Can You Give Jesus to?

We are commissioned by God to share Jesus. Do you remember who first shared Jesus with you? For me, it was one of the first neighbors I met when we moved into a new area. I believe it was a divine setup. She

was the only Christian on that street, as far as I knew, and there were actually others who spoke negatively of her. (Satan's scheme, I'm sure.) I am so grateful that she shared Jesus in a gentle manner. She shared about God's unconditional love and showed me how to grow my faith in him through church and Bible studies. I have learned to share my faith, letting people know they can receive Jesus just as they are. Too many people see themselves as unworthy, but he comes as a precious gift with no strings attached. It's an eternal, unconditional gift, waiting to be unwrapped. Who do you know who needs the gift of Jesus?

> Freely you have received, freely give. (Matthew 10:8)

> For the wages of sin is death, but the gift of God is eternal life in Christ Jesus our Lord. (Romans 6:23)

July 21

Discern God's Gentle Nudge

It's sometimes hard to discern when God is disciplining you. Many go through trials from beginning to end without knowing it's all about them. When we understand that God is trying to get our attention and focus on the leading of the Holy Spirit, we can forego those harsh days. Ask God to fill you with the fruit of the Holy Spirit, and claim his promises every day. Remember, the Holy Spirit gently leads; Satan rushes in. Most good things don't come from a hurried spirit. God is gently knocking at your door; get up, go to the door, and let him in.

> The fear of the Lord is the beginning of knowledge, but fools despise wisdom and discipline. (Proverbs 1:7)

> Those whom I love I rebuke and discipline. (Revelation 3:19)

July 22

If You Don't Boldly Stand for Something You Will Fall for Anything

In order to stand, we must first sit in the hands of our Lord and Savior with confidence that he will sustain us. After we have put all our trust in him, we can stand on his promises and know we will not fall for the devil's schemes. Asking God to fill you each morning with the Holy Spirit will give you the power of discernment to be strong and bold in whatever circumstance. We need to know who our directions come from. If it is Satan, he will tempt us to follow a road that leads nowhere. Don't fall for his tactics. Be strong, be bold, for the Lord thy God is with you!

> And they were all filled with the Holy Spirit and spoke the word of God boldly. (Acts 4:31)

> When I called, you answered me; you greatly emboldened me. (Psalm 138:3)

July 23

Don't Fast to Earn Something from God; Fast to Connect with God

In the book of Matthew, the first scripture regarding fasting (Matthew 6:16) says, "*When* you fast," not "*if* you fast." It says your heavenly Father will reward you if you keep your fast a secret from others. It's so much better to receive recognition from God than praise from the world. If you are looking for guidance or an answer to prayer, go ahead and fast silently. Fasting can be going without a certain meal for a day or as long as a few days or a week. Use the time you would have spent eating to connect with God. Seek his will, ask for direction, pray for healing, or just sit and listen. He will speak to you through your thoughts, others, and scripture. Look for his blessings; they are everywhere! After fasting in secret, your Father, who has seen what you did, will reward you. How awesome is that?

So that it will not be obvious to men that you are fasting, but only to your Father, who is unseen; and your Father, who sees what is done in secret, will reward you. (Matthew 6:18)

July 24

Christians Are Not Better, Just Better Off!

We are better off because of what Jesus did for us, but we are not loved more, for God loves everyone the same. The reason we are better off is because Christ in our life is a compass to guide our day. If you don't have a personal relationship with God, you start your day with a plan that doesn't include his will. He died for us so we can spend eternity with him in heaven. He has a specific plan for each one of us, and that compass will help us live out that plan. We will have God's peace. As Proverbs 14:30 says, "A heart at peace gives life to the body." That's why we're better off!

July 25

God's Created Order Is the Marriage of One Man to One Woman

So on the fifth day of the seven days of creation, God created male and female to come together as one to reproduce and fill the earth with people for him to love and for them to love him in return. It is clear that God's perfect order for marriage is between one man and one woman. The book of Matthew says a man will leave his mother and father (a man and a woman) and be united to his wife. That would be a man with a woman, not a man with a man or a woman with a woman. If a man or woman prefers to be with someone of the same sex, he or she can do so and even have a ceremony uniting them. But they can't call it marriage. The definition of marriage can't be changed to suit a changing culture.

In the beginning the Creator "made them male and female," and said, "For this reason a man will leave his father and mother and be united to his wife, and the two will become one flesh." So,

they are no longer two, but one. Therefore, what God has joined together, let man not separate. (Matthew 19:4–6)

God blessed them and said to them, "Be fruitful and increase in number; fill the earth and subdue it." (Genesis 1:28)

July 26

Don't Mistake Decency for Holiness

Decency—conforming to the commonly expected standards of good behavior (having to do with man). Knowing about God in the mind.

Holiness—separate unto God, purity, godliness (having to do with God). Knowing about God in the heart.

Our fundamental purpose is to follow Jesus. He actually commands us to be holy. How do we become holy? Keep seeking him and moving toward him. Stay on his path and always seek his absolute truth. When we stop moving, we become stale and ineffective for his purpose. If we stop moving, it becomes about us and not about him.

But just as he who called you is holy, so be holy in all you do; for it is written: "Be holy, because I am holy." (1 Peter 1:15–16)

Make every effort to live in peace with all men and to be holy; without holiness no one will see the Lord. (Hebrews 12:14)

July 27

Bridling the Tongue Is a Matter of the Heart

Can you attest to this as well as I can? I am ashamed of how often I have gossiped or gotten angry with someone. A damaging word will continue

to damage even though you apologize. Words ring loud and clear and can haunt someone even if they have forgiven you. Our tongue was given for one purpose only: to praise God's name. If you remember that Jesus died for that person you are talking about, you will show the same mercy to them that God continually shows you.

> Out of the overflow of the heart the mouth speaks. (Matthew 12:34)

> May the words of my mouth and the meditation of my heart be pleasing in your sight, oh Lord, my Rock and my Redeemer. (Psalm 19:14)

July 28

What Comes in Must Come Out

We've all heard the phrase, "Garbage in, garbage out." We can also say, "God's word in, God's word out." Mercy received, mercy given. What we hear we eventually speak. It's all a matter of the heart. Pray for a Jesus-infused heart. On the Day of Judgment, you will have to answer to him for how your heart spoke.

> For out of the overflow of the mouth, the heart speaks. (Matthew 12:34)

> The good man brings good things out of the good stored up in him, and the evil man brings evil things out of the evil stored up in him. (Matthew 12:35)

July 29

If on Trial for Being a Christian, Would You be Convicted?

My Christian friends would probably convict me only because I am usually on my best behavior when I am with them. It's much easier to show kindness and mercy when you like the person you're with and all things appear to be going well. However, it's very difficult to turn the other cheek when you are with someone unlovable and an offensive situation comes up. Knowing Jesus as your personal Savior is the best remedy for this. The closer you get to him, the better chance you will be convicted. I have a fish emblem on my car, which means I am a Christian. But how many times have I cursed another driver and given Jesus a bad name? Maybe I should put a fish on my forehead so I will see it in the rearview mirror!

Blessed are you when people insult you, persecute you and falsely say all kinds of evil against you because of me. (Matthew 4:11)

Do not be overcome by evil, but overcome evil with good. (Romans 12:21)

July 30

It Takes Twenty Days to Make or Break a Habit

Habit: a behavior pattern acquired by frequent repetition
(Merriam-Webster Dictionary)

I was in the habit of starting an exercise program on Monday and quitting on Tuesday. One day in a row, right? When I finally understood that I would need to exercise twenty days in a row to see results, I felt I could see the light at the end of the tunnel. I chose a habit I thought you could relate to, but you can fill in the blank regarding your own habits, whether good or bad. Never give up; the outcome far outweighs the pain. Don't

forget to ask for God's help, and when the twenty days are up, don't forget to thank him.

The twenty days relates to many other things, like prayer, trying to stop smoking, etc. It all takes discipline. Give it a try. You will have accomplished something to be proud of, and then you can start on the next thing. Always count on God to help.

> Do not throw away your confidence; it will be richly rewarded. You need to persevere so that when you have done the will of God, you will receive what he has promised. (Hebrews 10:35–36)

July 31

Our Habits Affect Our Happiness

I have a confession to make. Exercising for twenty days in a row never happened for me! I did, however, get in the habit of walking on my treadmill three times a week for several months. That counts, right? You have to do what works for you. You might be wondering why I chose this particular habit as my example. I hesitated using it because I was thinking there's nothing spiritual about this activity. Nor does it glorify God. But then the Holy Spirit reminded me that my body is a temple of God and that it is my responsibility to keep myself healthy. The walking, nudge, and obedience affected me in a good way, and perhaps I inspired someone else. I was happy with the outcome. You will be too.

> Do you know that your body is a temple of the Holy Spirit, who is in you, whom you have received from God? You are not your own; you were bought at a price. Therefore honor God with your body. (1 Corinthians 6:19–20)

> Don't you know that you yourselves are God's temple and that God's Spirit dwells in your midst? (1Corinthians 3:16)

August 1

Having Ears Doesn't Mean
You Are Listening

Have you ever heard directly from God? I don't mean audibly but as a thought in your mind. Or maybe you've had a vision in your mind while praying. Oftentimes, God speaks to his people through his Holy Spirit. For instance, if you ask God to show you your sin, he will. He uses scripture, circumstances, other people, nature, our conscience, and much more. Our part is to keep our frequency tuned in, so to speak. Then when God gives us info, answers prayer, or reveals sin, we can hear him loud and clear. He expects you to listen. But you have to open those ears! Expect God to speak, and keep your antenna high!

He who has ears let him hear. (Matthew 11:15)

He who belongs to God hears what God says. (John 8:47)

August 2

What Does God Want You to Let Go Of?

Jesus once said to one of his disciples, "Sell all that you have and follow me" (Matthew 19:21). The disciple was sad because he was very rich and found treasure in his belongings. My understanding of this scripture, however, is not that the man had to sell everything, but rather he needed to understand what in his life was keeping him from giving 100% of himself to God.

If you have an idol in your life, whether it's a thing or a person, once you are obedient to giving it up, you can be assured God will replace it with something even better. Open your hands and let it go. Then wait in great expectation.

For where your treasure is there your heart is also. (Matthew 6:21)

August 3

Will Yourself to Love One Another

Have you ever had to ask God to help you love someone? Loving is actually a decision. Even though others might be different from us or have wronged us, we need to be obedient to God's greatest commandment, which is to love one another. Jesus died for that person as well as he died for you. Love means being willing to forgive. If we try to see others as Jesus sees them, the act of love is easy. Our will is the only thing God is not in control of, but the minute we ask him, he's right there for us. Remember, God loved us while we were yet sinners (Romans 5:8). We can do the same for others. Do unto others as you would have them do unto you (Luke 6:31).

This is my command, love one another. (John 15:17)

But the greatest of these is love. (1 Corinthians 13:13)

August 4

If Jesus Pushed the Throttle Forward, Would You be ready?

Moving a throttle forward on a machine speeds it up, sometimes with a jolt. If you are not hanging on, you could get thrown off. Maybe you decided not to fasten the seat belt or weren't aware of the bumps and gullies in the road. Maybe you were able to dust yourself off and get right back on, or perhaps you injured yourself and needed to call for help. If Jesus pushed the throttle of your life suddenly forward, would you be able to stay your course? Could you stay afloat and ride the wave? If we have Jesus Christ as our safety net, we may experience the bumps and gullies, but we will always be able to hold on and resume our position again.

Be alert and always keep on praying. (Ephesians 6:18)

Pay attention and gain understanding. (Proverbs 4:1)

August 5

Christianity Is the Only Religion That Deals with Your Past

In other religions there is something you have to do to earn your way to heaven. It's totally up to you to get there or there isn't any heaven at all. In Christianity, making Jesus the Lord of your life is your ticket to heaven and it has been paid for. Romans 8:1 says, "Therefore, there is no condemnation for those who are in Christ Jesus." In other words, you do nothing. Being saved is not the result of good works; however, good works are characteristic of one who has been saved. If your place of worship teaches something other than salvation through Jesus, do some research and learn how and why Jesus died for you. The truth will set you free!

> For it is by grace you have been saved, through faith—and this is not of yourselves, it is the gift of God—not by works, so that no one can boast. (Ephesians 2:8)

> Know the truth and the truth will set you free. (John 8:32)

August 6

Don't Pick up the Devil's Bundles

Have you ever been convicted of something you have been doing? Is there something, someone, or somewhere in your life God has forbidden you? Sometimes it's tempting to make excuses or to justify why it's probably "okay this time." Satan drops those little bundles in our pathway hoping to make us stumble. If we drop our guard for even a minute and decide to take a peek under the covered bundle, the victory may be his. When you are tempted, stand firm and praise God and the devil will flee. It's all about temptation and how God's power can help you overcome.

> Resist the devil and he will flee from you. (James 4:7)

And no wonder, for Satan himself masquerades as an angel of light. (2Corinthians 11:14)

August 7

Partial Love Is No Love at All

Partial love is no love.
Partial goodness is no goodness.
Partial patience is no patience.
Partial forgiveness is no forgiveness.

Jesus never held back any part of himself. Imagine Jesus only forgiving part of our sins. What if he only gave us part of his grace? What if we only had part of a relationship with him? Would we only have a portion of salvation and a fraction of the inheritance of heaven? So should we hold back any part of ourselves, giving only partial obedience or partial love to him or others? Give wholly to others as Christ has given to you, and through that act, you will be obedient to his calling. Fully obedient.

> Jesus relied, "If anyone loves me he will obey my teaching." (John 14:23)

August 8

"Be Holy Because I Am Holy"
1Peter 1:16

Are we born holy? Because of Adam and Eve's sin in the Garden of Eden, we need to be born twice before the process of holiness begins; once physically by our mothers and once spiritually by God. Do we need to *try* to be holy? When we first give ourselves to the Lord, we crave pure spiritual milk like newborn babies to nourish us in our walk with him. When we taste that the Lord is good, we want to be like him. I don't believe we need to *try* to become holy as he is holy; it is a process through which the Holy Spirit guides us. Humility keeps us from thinking we have reached that goal. The minute we think we are holy, we are not.

In reply Jesus declared, "I tell you the truth, no one can see the kingdom of God unless he is born again." (John 3:7)

August 9

Meekness: Strength under Control

Jesus was the epitome of meekness. He was a lamb slaughtered for his obedience to God. He set an example of gentle strength and humility. We can include in our prayers to have an attitude like Jesus, but don't get discouraged when you can't live up to it. The fact that you desire meekness is in direct obedience to God, and he will bless you for it. It's a form of spiritual bodybuilding—from the inside out.

Blessed are the meek for they shall inherit the earth. (Matthew 5:5)

The beauty of a gentle and quiet spirit. (1 Peter 3:4)

August 10

The Hole in the Street

Have you ever hoped for a better outcome without changing your current strategy? One of the definitions of insanity is doing the same thing over and over again and expecting different results. If at first you don't succeed, try, try again, right? Maybe you just need to tweak your plan a little. This could refer to a relationship, a destination, a school grade, perhaps your garden, employment, or anything in which you desire to see a change. If every time you go to a friend's house you end up in a pothole, don't wait for the pothole to be fixed. Take a different route! Don't rely on someone else to make things better. You are in charge of your own outcome. With God's help, you can find a newly paved street without all the barriers to dodge. Don't settle for less than what God wants to give you! Trust and obey!

Teach me to do your will for you are my God. May your good spirit lead me on level ground. (Psalm 143:10)

August 11

It Is Good to be Held Accountable

Have you ever asked someone to hold you accountable regarding your personal walk with the Lord? It's a good practice to have a close friend as your accountability partner; one who will keep it confidential. Many of us set boundaries for ourselves; many of us have them set by someone else, like our mother when we were young or a spouse later in life. If those boundaries are broken and sin results, being held accountable will help get you back on track. If you are the accountability partner, always remember to restore gently and with love as God does with us. It's a tough job to be held accountable. Be ready and open to hear what the other has to say.

> If someone is caught in a sin, you who are spiritual should restore him gently. (Galatians 6:1–2)

> A cord of three strands is not easily broken. (Ecclesiastes 4:12)

The last passage refers to your accountability partner, God, and you.

August 12

Stay the Course and the Lord Will Give His Grace

Grace is similar to receiving a drop of water when you're thirsty, a pebble of food when you are starving, or help on the evening your car breaks down. Gratitude rises up from the lowest ventricle of your heart and you feel indebted for life. You wonder, how can I ever pay them back? What about the day you learned your sin helped nail Jesus to the cross? He took your place and paid the price for your sin just because he loved you. You didn't have to do anything to receive that grace. You didn't even have to ask! There is nothing we can add to what Jesus did for us because it's all grace. He gives it to us way before we know we are in need of it. So don't give up; his grace will always be sufficient for you (2 Corinthians 12:9). He said so!

Let us then approach the throne of grace with confidence, so that we may receive mercy to help us in our time of need. (Hebrews 4:16)

August 13

Listen with Faith

We begin listening the moment we are born; perhaps even when inside our mother's womb. As a child growing up, we are taught to listen for many reasons: to learn, to be safe, to discern and for our pleasure. We trust that the things we listen to are for our own good. When we come to the age of reason, we are sometimes left on our own to decide what and who we will listen to. In the verses below, we are told to listen to God's instructions in his word. Proverbs 4:20–22 says these instructions are life and health to our bodies. So live by faith, not by sight.

Let the wise listen and add to their learning and let the discerning get guidance. (Proverbs 1:5)

The way of a man seems right to him but a wise man listens to advice. (Proverbs 12:15)

August 14

Praying Out Loud and Giving God Glory

When we pray out loud for someone or over someone, the risk is God's, not ours. If we are led to pray, and are praying in the will of God, we need to have faith that God will see it through. But always resist the temptation to take the glory from God. There are certain songs that have an awakening effect on me. "To God Be the Glory," is one of them. All things are to God's glory; therefore, always beware of exalting yourself. Everything good that we think or do is from God. The blessing is for us, but the glory is his. Even faith is a gift of the Holy Spirit, given to us by God. Thank him for it each time you pray.

Whatever you do, do it for the glory of God. (1 Corinthians 10:31)

His praise will continually be on my lips. (Psalm 34:1)

August 15

What You Depend On isn't Enough ... Unless It's Jesus

Some people go through their entire lives trying to figure things out. Proverbs is full of scripture regarding the benefits of knowing and following God's teachings. Proverbs describes wisdom as being more precious than rubies and more profitable than silver or gold. We should always strive to make straight paths for ourselves, but if we should fall and go our own way, God will always have his arms stretched toward us, ready to pick us up, brush us off, and help us start all over again. Start every day asking Jesus what he wants to accomplish through you that day. You will need to choose him because he will not force himself into your life.

Trust in the Lord with all your heart. Lean not on you own understanding. In all your ways acknowledge him and he will make your paths straight. (Proverbs 3:5–6)

August 16

Humility Does Not Negate Self-Worth

If we have accepted the gift of Jesus and therefore have God's spirit within us, we can be humble and still enjoy personal merit. Just because we are happy with the outcome of our goal doesn't mean we are full of human pride. Pride is having a sense of personal dignity, a feeling of pleasure because of something achieved. Humility means meekness or modesty. We can be proud of our good grades in college or of our children, but we can't take credit for them. We can feel good about ourselves and still remain humble if we give God the glory and thank him for it.

Be humble and gentle in spirit. (Matthew 11:29)

Whatever you do, do it all for the glory of God and you will find rest for your souls. (1 Corinthians 10:31)

August 17

Pray to Become What God Desires

Have you ever wondered what your spiritual gifts are or tried to figure out why you're at a certain place at a particular time in your life? God has a specific plan for you and already knows how your life will turn out. He knew you before you were born. (Read Psalm 139:13–16.) Even though he gives us free will to make choices, he knows way ahead of time which road we will choose. A good habit to get into is asking God every morning to show you what it is he wants you to accomplish that day. Ask to be his vessel and an instrument of his peace. Let him use you to further his kingdom. And to God be the glory!

> That he who began a good work in you will carry it on to completion until the day of Christ Jesus. (Philippians 1:6)

August 18

Sometimes Denials Are In Our Best Interest

When you have time, read chapter 10 in the book of Daniel. You will learn that God's wisdom for Daniel was delayed for twenty-one days. It is one of the most profound scriptures regarding God's perfect timing. If you have ever tried to help God move on something specific, you know what I am talking about. God knows just what he is doing. You don't have to try to figure it all out. God will move all the playing pieces and allow circumstances to come to pass without any help from you. You are to simply trust and obey and stay out of the way. It may take years for an answer to a specific prayer because sometimes God is more interested in the process of getting there than he is in the outcome. That's called living life. Delays are not always denials!

He said to them, "it is not for you to know the times or dates the Father has set by his own authority." (Acts 1:7)

August 19

Is Your Cup Overflowing?

I'm drinking from my saucer because my cup is over flowing.
—John Paul Moore

What a beautiful thought to start each new day. Forget about what you do not have. It's about God's mercies and blessings he has bestowed on us. I agree that we seldom feel like this for very long. Why is that? I suppose it depends on who we are most filled with: the Holy Spirit or ourselves. Do you realize you already possess anything and everything you will ever need? Our most phenomenal possessions are God's mercy and his plentiful blessings. I'm quite sure that is the meaning of this phrase. It doesn't mean you are in a peaceful place and loving every minute of your day. It means you are enjoying God's peace amongst the chaos because that is the business he is in! Go ahead and taste the freedom that has been brewed for you.

I will send down showers in season; there will be showers of blessings. (Ezekiel 34:26)

The blessing of the Lord brings wealth (spiritual) and he adds no trouble to it. (Proverbs 10:22)

August 20

Refusing to Forgive is like
Swallowing Poison and Hoping
the Other Person Dies

We forgive because Christ forgave us (Matthew 18:33). I noticed in looking over the gifts of the Holy Spirit that forgiveness isn't one of them. The

list includes love, joy, peace, patience, kindness, goodness, gentleness, faithfulness, and self-control. However, I actually read "forgiveness" in every one of these. If you seek and possess any of these fruits, you can't possibly be unforgiving. Many people I looked up to over my lifetime appeared to possess all these traits. They were all God-loving, God-fearing people who knew the Holy Spirit as the giver of truth. Never did I see a spirit of unforgiveness in any of them. By forgiving someone, you not only set him or her free but, more importantly, you also set yourself free. My forgiveness of my father set both him and me free after many years of heartache. I was thankful for the opportunity to sit down and talk with him before he died. If you have someone to forgive, ask God to give you the strength and courage to do so. Throw the poison away and then enjoy the freedom!

Forgive as the Lord forgave you. (Colossians 3:13)

August 21

God Is the Lord of Your Circumstances

In the scriptures below, Paul is stating that he has learned to be content whatever the circumstances. Notice the word *learned*. Paul wasn't born that way—he only became content after realizing who was in charge of his circumstances. He learned that God would give him the strength to get through any difficult times. He says he knows what it is to be in need and what it is to have plenty. God provides for our needs through others. Paul calls the gifts from others a fragrant offering pleasing to God. It sounds like he had a grateful heart. Let us be thankful for whatever help, large or small, we receive from others and remember they will appreciate you also in their time of need. Let's depend on God for the unity between us and thank him for whatever our circumstances may be.

Give thanks in all circumstances for this is God's will for you. (1 Thessalonians 5:18)

August 22

Dance to the beat of a Different Drummer

I've often thought of dancing as a freedom kind of thing, where you just move and listen to the beat as you dance around the floor. However, it's interesting to note that not everyone seems to be hearing the same beat. It's like they don't care how everyone else is dancing; they only do what makes them feel good. I have a coaster from my mom that says, "Dance like there's nobody watching." This sounds like freedom to me. I get my freedom from Jesus Christ. Whose music are you dancing to?

> You turned my wailing into dancing. (Psalm 30:11)

> Let them praise his name with dancing. (Psalm 149:3)

August 23

Be a Link in the Chain

A gap in a fence results in weakness. Replacing the gap with a strong link will result in the best possible scenario. This is as an analogy for many situations, such as doing something good for our neighbor, giving up a seat on the bus, paying the change needed to complete another's grocery transaction, offering the last piece of your favorite pie to someone else, or devoting your life to service for your country. Large or small, it's a piece of you that helps make the world go 'round. I once was a volunteer at a nursing home where one elderly lady called me her angel from heaven. She said she was so blessed to have me visit, but I assured her the blessing was all mine. I guess you could say we were linked together. Be a rainbow in someone else's cloud.

> Let us not grow weary of doing good, for at the proper time we will reap a harvest if we do not give up. (Galatians 6:9)

August 24

Set the Table in Advance

You can be thankful for the answer to a prayer far in advance of any evidence that the answer is on its way. A good analogy would be inviting a friend for dinner, setting your table with your fine china and linens, and preparing a beautiful meal even though you haven't received the RSVP that the friend is coming. But you know that friend so well that it doesn't even cross your mind that he or she wouldn't show up. It's like putting the flag up on your mailbox or asking for a kiss good night from your three-year-old. Your expectations are the same every time. Without a doubt, you know your letter will be picked up and delivered and the embrace from your child will act like a sedative. We can always expect great things from God and should thank him in advance. Jesus thanked God for each of us before we were born. He knew we were coming!

Before I formed you in the womb I knew you. (Jeremiah 1:5)

He answered their prayer because they trusted him. (1 Chronicles 5:20)

August 25

Beware of Refusing to Go to the Funeral of Your own Independence

If we continually strive to keep our independence, we will never be conscious of our dependence on God. We need to understand the benefits of depending on him for everything. When we put God first in our lives, our focus is clear. The reason for the Ten Commandments was not that God expected us to keep them, but that we would become dependent on him and not ourselves. When we stop seeking after our own aspirations, God's intention for us will become our desire. The desire for our independence is actually a form of bondage. Bury your independence by giving it to God.

Teach me to do your will for you are my God; may your good spirit lead me on level ground. (Psalm 143:10)

Be still and know that I am God. (Psalm 46:10)

August 26

Oil Hinges with Kindness

You have no doubt heard the adage, "What goes around comes around," or the golden rule, "Do unto others what you would have them do unto you." Although there are times when our kindness backfires, most often it benefits others and us. Even Jesus' kindness didn't always pay off, but he told us to turn the other cheek in those situations. Kindness is one of the fruits of the Holy Spirit. The best kindness is when we aren't even trying. As Luke 6:38 says, "Give and it will be given to you. A good measure, pressed down, shaken together and running over, will be poured into your lap. For with the measure you use, it will be measured to you." Don't let the hinges become rusty.

> Be kind and compassionate to one another, forging each other, just as in God, Christ forgave you. (Ephesians 4:32)

August 27

Reminded of the Past so We Don't Trust in the Future

Can you remember a time when you thought you could fix a bad situation by manipulating and maneuvering to flawlessly set the stage? How did it end up? Not the way you planned, huh? Did you make things worse? Did you ruin any friendships? Did you learn anything from it? Hopefully, you have learned not to trust in your own wisdom by remembering the outcome. Trusting only in God will reserve a good place in the future. Let God lead the way. He will help you not repeat those mistakes again. Remember the past as a valuable teacher, but don't live there.

Trust in the Lord with all your heart and lean not on your own understanding; in all your ways acknowledge him, and he will make your paths straight. (Proverbs 3:5–6)

August 28

Passing Judgment on Those Weaker Than Us

Being judgmental about anything is oftentimes hypocritical. Matthew says we sometimes have the urge to take the speck out of another's eye when we actually have a plank in our own eye (Matthew 7:3). And in many instances, the particular thing we dislike in that person is something we dislike in ourselves. We need to work on fixing ourselves first before we can see clearly to help someone else. Many of the differences we find in others are disputable and not worth the words and energy. Don't look down on your brother. Seek to find your way and then you can lead him to truth. Everyone needs the encouragement of the scriptures to satisfy the hope in his or her soul. In this, God can be glorified.

> Accept him who is weak, without passing judgement on disputable matters. (Romans 14:1)

Do not judge, or you too will be judged. For in the same way you judge others, you will be judged, and with the measure you use, it will be measured to you. Why do you look at the speck of sawdust in your brother's eye and pay no attention to the plank in your own eye? How can you say to your brother, 'Let me take the speck out of your eye,' when all the time there is a plank in your own eye? You hypocrite, first take the plank out of your own eye, and then you will see clearly to remove the speck from your brother's eye. (Matthew 7:1–5)

August 29

The Power of a Renewed Mind

Morning brings a whole new perspective, doesn't it? Most often we wake up refreshed and with energy and confidence to face the world. But just a word of caution: don't go past the threshold without God in your pocket. You will need his power to keep your thoughts obedient to Christ. With the power of a renewed mind, we can do all things through Christ who strengthens us (Philippians 4:13). Even before your feet touch the floor in the morning, before you greet anyone in your household, meet with God. Lay your requests before him, and wait in expectation. Seek him and his kingdom and all things will be opened unto you (Matthew 6:33).

> In the morning, oh Lord, you hear my voice: in the morning I lay my requests before you and wait in expectation. (Psalm 5:3)

> And we take captive every thought to make it obedient to Christ. (2 Corinthians 10:5)

August 30

Grief Is an Open Secret

Missing limbs, blindness, confinement to a wheelchair, and other scars are hard to hide. Possibly a great deal of our scars come from some type of tribulation or misfortune. However, although marred in some way, most of us make it through with flying colors. We carry the banner of victory. As Paul suffered in prison and Jonah inside the whale, if we trust in the power of God, we will end up undefeated and better for it. Paul went through so much suffering that he could say, "None of these things move me" (Acts 20:24). He was testifying to the gospel of God's grace. He finished the race and completed the task God set before him. He was a great example of perseverance. So no matter what you've been through, no matter how difficult it was, no matter the cost, know that Jesus was with you and it has all been for God's glory. Jesus carried many scars to the cross.

I know what it is to be in need, and I know what it is to have plenty. I have learned the secret of being content in any and every situation, whether well fed or hungry, whether living in plenty or in want. I can do everything through him who gives me strength. (Philippians 4:12–13)

August 31

Make Me a Channel of Your Peace

Soon after Susan Boyle won on *Britain's Got Talent,* her first Christmas CD was released, *The Gift.* After listening to it endlessly, I went back to the store and purchased one for each of my sisters and a couple of friends. I'm not sure if it touched them the way it did me, but it is at the top of my favorites. One of the songs, "Make Me a Channel of Your Peace," asks to be used by God. Some of the verses are as follows:

> Where there is hatred let me bring your love …
> Where there is injury—your pardon Lord.
> When there is doubt—true faith in you …
> Where there is despair in life—let me bring hope.
> Where there is darkness—only light …
> Where there is sadness—ever joy.
>
> Oh Master, grant that I may never seek
> To be consoled—as to console,
> To be understood—as to understand,
> To be loved—as to love with all my soul.
> It is in pardoning that we are pardoned
> In giving to all men, that we receive,
> And in dying, we are born to eternal life.

Peacemakers who sow in peace raise a harvest of righteousness. (James 3:18)

For he himself is our peace, who has made the two one and has destroyed the barrier, the dividing wall of hostility. (Ephesians 2:14)

September 1

God sometimes withdraws His Gifts so You May Better Know and Love the Giver

There are times when we become too attached to material goods while believing they are gifts from God. Our God is a jealous God, and although he will give us the desires of our heart (Psalm 37:4), he will readily take them away if we enjoy the gift more than we enjoy him. In the Old Testament, God warns his people against any kind of idolatry. Any time something or someone causes you to compromise your love for God, don't be surprised if you feel a threat of it being removed. Your first devotion must be to Christ—no exceptions. He is the giver of life. When you love your life more than him, it is no longer his gift but your gift to yourself. We need to love the Giver more than the gift.

> You shall not make for yourself an image in the form of anything in heaven above or on the earth beneath or in the waters below. You shall not bow down to them or worship them; for I, the LORD your God, am a jealous God, punishing the children for the sin of the parents to the third and fourth generation of those who hate me, but showing love to a thousand generations of those who love me and keep my commandments. (Exodus 20:4-6)

September 2

You Can't Un-ring the Bell

Have you ever wished you could push rewind to delete a comment or action, maybe something that didn't come out the way you intended? I think this has happened to just about everyone. In our house, we always used the phrase "The milk is already spilled" when it was after the fact. Once the bell is rung, you can't un-ring it. Once the words are spoken, you can't take them back. Psalm 19:14 says, "May the words of my mouth and the meditation of my heart be pleasing in your sight, O Lord, my Rock and my Redeemer." Let the Holy Spirit be the guard over your mouth. It will help lessen your regrets.

A wise man's heart guides his mouth and his lips promote instruction. Pleasant words are a honeycomb, sweet to the soul and healing to the bones. (Proverbs 16:23–24)

September 3

It's *How* You Carry the Load That Breaks You

Did you know that 98 percent of the things we worry about never come to fruition? Yet the fear that something could happen breaks us down. Whether it's dealing with a personal problem or responsibility or carrying another's burden, it all comes back to having faith that God will be in the midst of things, bring you peace, and lead you in the right direction. This is all about how we deal with a problem or responsibility. Never take on a task without seeking God first. Then you can respond to trials and misgivings with peace of mind. Put all your eggs in one basket and give it to God.

> Carry each other's burdens, and in this way you will fulfill the law of Christ. (Galatians 6:2)

> But seek first his kingdom and his righteousness and all these things will be given to you as well. (Matthew 6:33)

September 4

Our God Is the Lord of the Harvest

God planted his garden in Eden and is awaiting the time of harvest. He has watered, fertilized, weeded, and cultivated it, and then let his Son shine down on it. As we enjoy the harvesting of our gardens in the fall, so God anxiously awaits his yield of believers. He is the Lord of the harvest and it's time for his helpers to come into the field and gather his crops. Will you say yes when he bids you to come? Gather the produce and bring it to the banquet table set for the King. God doesn't want to lose even one soul.

His Great Commission to us is to go out into all the nations and spread the good news. Looks like we should get busy!

> The harvest is plentiful but the workers are few. Ask the Lord of the harvest to send out workers into this harvest field. (Matthew 9:37–38)

> Let us not become weary in doing good, for at the proper time we will reap a harvest if we do not give up. (Galatians 6:9)

September 5

People Notice When God Is in Your Life

How often have you met someone for the first time and felt as though he or she knew God? You probably noticed his or her gentle, quiet spirit. Did he or she seem harmonized with life and show contentment and peace? Shortly after becoming a Christian, I wanted to be that person. I especially prayed for a quiet, gentle spirit and for deliverance from a sometimes harsh tongue. It's been over forty years now, and I've come to the conclusion that God isn't finished with me yet. When you want to please God with the things you say and do, you really need to be attentive to the Holy Spirit and put him first in your life. You never know when your behavior could be the link that puts someone in touch with God.

> Your beauty should not come from outward adornment, such as braided hair and the wearing of gold jewelry and fine clothes. Instead, it should be that of your inner self, the unfading beauty of a gentle and quiet spirit, which is of great worth in God's sight. (1 Peter 3:3–4)

> Finally, all of you, live in harmony with one another; be sympathetic, love as brothers, be compassionate and humble. (1 Peter 3:8)

September 6

Riches can be a Blessing from God

Often people believe they have riches because they worked hard to get them and somehow deserve them. This is called entitlement. God gives us the ability to produce wealth (Deuteronomy 8:18). Did you know that? The reason he gives wealth is so we would share with those less fortunate. It's not usually about us, although we may wish it were. He will give us the desires of our heart physically and spiritually, but only when we are obedient to him. When we accept the riches from him, they have a deeper and lasting meaning. Matthew 6:33 says, "Seek first his kingdom and his righteousness, and all these things will be given to you as well." Seek him, know him, and love him. Then receive and give it away!

> All these blessings will come upon you and accompany you if you obey the Lord your God. (Deuteronomy 28:2)

> Moreover, when God gives any man wealth and possessions, and enables him to enjoy them, to accept his lot and be happy in his work—this is a gift from God. (Ecclesiastes 5:19)

September 7

The Lord Is with You even when you don't feel Him

God never moves away from you. He is a jealous God and loves spending time with you. If you aren't feeling his presence, you might want to examine your prayer life. If you are counting on the Sunday service to fill you, with no time set aside for God during the week, you may be missing many of God's blessings. Take time to get into the presence of God. Open yourself to him, and let him fill you to overflowing. Do it in the morning if you can and start off with your tank filled for the day. He has so much more in store for you than you know. Stay close and walk in his light.

He went out to meet Asa and said to him, "Listen to me Asa and all Judah and Benjamin. The Lord is with you when you are with him. If you seek him, he will be found by you; but if you forsake him, he will forsake you." (2 Chronicles 15:2)

Blessed are those who have learned to acclaim you, who walk in the light of your presence O Lord. (Psalm 89:15)

September 8

"Man Is Destined to Die Once"
(Hebrews 9:27)

Do you know anyone who believes in reincarnation? The above scripture and the one below negate that 100 percent. If you read on through Hebrews 10, you will see for yourself that Christ died once for us and we will only die once. If we were coming back to a second life, wouldn't Jesus have to come back and die all over again for us? The only reason Jesus is coming a second time is to take us to heaven where he has prepared a place for us for eternity (John 14:2). That is a promise of Jesus, and you can count on it. Enjoy this life you've been given and live it to the fullest for God's purpose. That's why he created you, and you only have this one chance. Life is not a dress rehearsal!

And if I go and prepare a place for you I will come back and take you to be with me, that you also will be where I am. (John 14:2)

September 9

The Bible Says Marriage Is between
One Man and One Woman

It is very difficult to write on this subject without coming across as judgmental. I believe it is God's job to judge. In the scriptures below it's inconceivable that God could mean anything other than for one man and one woman to live as one flesh in the sacrament he created called

marriage. The reproductive system works that way. It's not a theory. It was a command from God to be fruitful and increase in number. His purpose of creation was for his pleasure. He wanted to fill the earth with people he could love and be loved by in return. God says those who indulge in sexual sin and in many other sins will not inherit the kingdom of God. One must choose to serve God or him- or herself. God loves the sinner but hates the sin. Ask God to lead you in his intended direction.

God created man. He created both male and female (Genesis 1:7).

"He blessed them and said, 'Be fruitful and increase in number; fill the earth and subdue it'" (Genesis 1:28).

God created man (Genesis 2:7).

God made a helper suitable for him (Genesis 2:18).

God made woman from Adam's rib (Genesis 2:21–22).

Man leaves father and mother and man and woman become one flesh (Genesis 2:24).

"Some of you were sinners. But you were washed and were sanctified (made holy) ... by Jesus" (1 Corinthians 6:9).

The fifth of the Ten Commandments says, "Obey your father and your mother" (Deuteronomy 5:16).

September 10

"Bad Company Corrupts good Character"
(1 Corinthians 15:33)

If we move those words around a little we can also say that good company can change bad character, right? If you put an alcoholic and a priest together in the same room for a week, what do you get? Two drunken priests! Jesus wants us to impart the good from our souls to those who need his love. It will take strength to overpower corrupt behavior. If we are to

win souls for God, we need to let his light shine through us. They will feel the warmth of his love and will receive the new life offered.

September 11

If Freedom Comes from Man, Man can also take It Away

God is always on his throne. Look to him for understanding, and strive to be under his rule. Men quite often change the rules to suit themselves. Think about how man's rules have changed over time. Our country was founded on the basis of Christianity, and it has sufficed for years. Now people in government and in other organizations forbid the Ten Commandments to be displayed in public. There can no longer be prayer in school, and kids are not allowed to have their "meet you at the flag" sessions. Abortion is legal in most cases and states, and there are those who use it as a form of birth control. Marriage is no longer specifically between one man and one woman. The sanctity of marriage has been denied. This is a direct hit on God and it flows over onto God's people. All of a sudden, the Constitution is questioned and many want it amended to suit their needs. It is no longer a government by and for the people but a government for itself. When we obey God and live as he created us to live, we receive his blessings (Deuteronomy 28). I'm not saying Christians don't encounter troubles, only that when they do they have a better response to life. God goes through everything with you and gives you peace when you ask for it. Don't give your freedom away. Stand up for God.

> The Lord has established his throne in heaven, and his kingdom rules over all. (Psalm 103:19)

> If my people, who are called by my name, will humble themselves and pray and seek my face and turn from their wicked ways, then I will hear from heaven, and I will forgive their sin and will heal their land. (2 Chronicles 7:14)

September 12

Never Measure Yourself with Yourself

If you needed an accurate measurement, would you use a broken yardstick? No matter how many times you measured, it would be a false measurement. We would need a perfect yardstick. Human measurements are also faulty. We cannot leave God out of the equation. We cannot boast about what we have done but only what God has done through us. When we boast to others, we receive our reward from them and not from God. Also, God is the one we should look to, to fill us up. It's only important what he thinks of us, not others. God calls us the salt of the earth and the light of the world (Matthew 5:13–14). He sees us from the inside out. Use God's yardstick if you want a true measurement of yourself.

> For they loved praise from men more than praise from God. (John 12:43)

> Be sure not to display your "acts of righteousness" before men, to be seen by them. If you do, you will have no reward from your Father in heaven. (Matthew 6:1)

September 13

Loving the Unlovely

Jesus gives us many examples of how to love the unlovely. He had ample compassion for lepers, his persecutors, and those who crucified him. When God gave us the command to love one another, he didn't say to do so only if the circumstances are acceptable to us. Loving your neighbor as yourself covers a lot of ground. Being around a relative who rubs you the wrong way is most often extremely difficult. A co-worker who doesn't shower regularly can be disgusting. The loud, obnoxious, lazy person needs love; he just doesn't know that it's free from Jesus; unconditional and unending. God so loved the world that he gave his Son to save us (John 3:16). Even though the world was and still is quite unlovely, God is not giving up on us. He waits patiently.

Jesus replied, "Love the Lord your God with all your heart, soul, and mind. This is the first and greatest commandment. And the second is like it: love your neighbor as yourself." (Matthew 22:37–39)

September 14

Jesus Christ Is the Gate

When you see a fence with a gate do you ever wonder what the gate represents? Is the gate there to keep someone or something in, or is it there to keep someone or something out? Most beautiful gardens that are of some value are gated. Gates protect it from intruders and lay out a boundary. A gate sometimes indicates a plot of land that is carefully cultivated. Sometimes you see signs that say "Keep Out" or "No Trespassing" on the gate, daring you to enter. I think Jesus' gate would have a sign that says "Welcome" and a big spotlight showing the way. Jesus says, "This is the way, walk in it" (Isaiah 31:21). He calls us to pass through the gate and enter into his care. He never forces us to enter; he wants us to come of our own free will. He beckons us, saying, "I am the way the truth and the life" (John 14:16) and "I am the gate; whoever enters through me will be saved" (John10:9). So when Jesus opens a gate for you, walk through in confidence that his way will lead to the Father. Let him weed, water, and fertilize you for the maximum output for him to enjoy. You are put on this earth for his pleasure.

> He has brought you down the narrow road that leads to the gate that gives life. Only a few find it! If you are faithful to God in your present situation he will take care of your future. (Matthew 7:13)

September 15

Freedom from Whatever

Phillips, Craig & Dean sing a song called "This Is How It Feels to Be Free." The lyrics relate to a guy who was feeling like he was in prison—a living nightmare burning deep within. His chains fell off, and he tasted

freedom—and won't go back again. It's quite a story of redemption. This is, of course, an analogy of what it feels like to know God. Not just knowing about God but having a personal relationship with him through the mercy of Jesus. John 8:32 says, "Know the truth and the truth will set you free." When Jesus rose from the dead and walked again with his disciples, he told them he would send a comforter, the Holy Spirit, who would guide them into all truth (John 16:13). That truth, if we listen to it, will result in our freedom. Then you will want to tell others, "This is what it means to be free" from whatever you were in bondage to!

> Now the Lord is the Spirit, and where the Spirit of the Lord is, there is freedom. (2 Corinthians 3:17)

September 16

Purity: Far Too Deep to Arrive at Naturally

The only way we can ever be pure, according to God's definition, is by giving ourselves totally to Jesus. We can get up every morning and tell ourselves that today will be different. Today I will work on cleaning up my act. So we go out into the world and look something like bumper cars at the State Fair or the waves on a white-capped lake. We attempt to dodge those who get in our way and think that riding the wave will enable us to give ourselves a happy-face sticker at the end of the day. But our day will end with yet another failed attempt to be all that we think we should be. And we say again, "Tomorrow will be different. I'll work on that thing called purity." Let the Holy Spirit guide you throughout the day. Ask God what he wants you to accomplish and what will bring him glory. Because when God is glorified you are blessed. I think it's a matter of the heart.

> Who can say I have kept my heart pure; I am clean and without sin. (Proverbs 20:9)

> Create in me a pure heart Oh God and renew a steadfast spirit in me. (Psalm 15:10)

September 17

If My People . . .

If my people who are called by my name, will humble themselves and pray and seek my face and turn from their wicked ways, then will I hear from heaven and will forgive their sin and will heal their land. (2 Chronicles 7:14)

Please forgive us, Lord, for these things:

- living together before marriage
- same-sex partners
- same-sex marriages
- sex changes
- child abuse
- child molestation
- pornography
- executive greed
- drug and alcohol abuse
- the word *God* taken out of schools and government centers
- wars, killing in the name of God and Allah
- immorality
- infidelity
- children killing children
- children killing parents
- abusing POWs
- immoral and unethical use of the Internet
- abortion
- corrupt governments

The list goes on and on . . .

September 18

Waiting for Hope

There is a very fine line, a thin veil that hides a glimpse of heaven from us when we are in a dark place. When you find a particular circumstance as hopeless, you can be sure that God sees things quite the opposite on the other side of the veil. He is that close! At times, things seem so bad that we don't even know what to pray for. So we pray for the hope that our dilemma will soon end and we will see a slight image of his face through the veil and know he is there. Hope is to wish for something with a feeling of confident expectation. Don't ever give up on it. It's where faith comes from. Hold on until God turns your hope into a reality.

Though he slay me, yet will I hope in him. (Job 13:15)

But those who hope in the Lord will renew their strength. (Isaiah 40:31)

September 19

Not *Deserving* of Happiness, But *Worthy* of Happiness

Don't block your blessings because you believe you don't deserve them. Jesus thinks you are worth it! That's why he was willing to accept the cup his Father gave him to drink. Jesus didn't die for us because we deserved it. Just the opposite! His death was our mercy. You show mercy and forgive someone because you love him or her and feel he or she is worth forgiving and having a relationship with. Even though many of us don't feel worthy of God's gift of forgiveness and the comfort of the Holy Spirit, you *must* believe that Jesus' sacrifice wipes away your stain of sin. God has washed you white as snow because of his unconditional love. Don't try to be worthy; God already made you that way.

A happy heart makes the face cheerful. (Proverbs 15:13)

September 20

Everyone Needs Validation

"Do you see me? Do you hear me? Does anything I say matter to you?"

Those around you can't forever validate you. Most of the world is too busy patting themselves on the back. When everything is going right for them, they might pull you up by your bootstraps, but don't count on it. God sees you and hears you, and everything you do matters to him. He is the only one who will always be there for you. It as if the day you came out of your mother's womb your forehead was stamped "Validated." You can probably get some validation from others, but it will never be sufficient. Live your life for an audience of the One! You'll get applause every time.

> Trust in the Lord with all your heart and lean not on your own understanding. (Proverbs 3:5)

September 21

Laziness Never Results in Prosperity

Do you know any circumstance that holds true to this proverb? Family? Friends? Neighbors? Do you ever get tired of watching those around you keep doing the same thing over and over again and expecting different results? They always find something or someone else to blame for their situation. They play the blame game but never win.

I understand God's command to give to those in need. That's called a blessing. But when we continue to bail others out of a self-inflicted predicament, we become enablers and they will never learn to stand on their own. They need to learn to lean on God, not us. Let him be their Savior. He's better at it!

> Lazy hands make a man poor, but diligent hands bring wealth. (Proverbs 10:4)

We do not want you to become lazy, but to imitate those who through faith and patience inherit what has been promised. (Hebrews 6:12)

September 22

Your Life Is Speaking to You. What Is It Saying?

I'm sure you believe that God speaks to you through his word and through others. Are you open to what others say in regard to your life? Sometimes the Holy Spirit reveals things to us. Are you being still enough to hear that quiet movement? Do you sit in church and wish so and so were there to hear this or that? Or could the sermon be directed specifically to you? Do you learn from your mistakes or do you play the blame game? Do you ask God to show you your sin, and then just when it's becoming clear, you look the other way? God knows your heart. Let him show you the life he wants you to have. Be still so you can hear the gentle brush of his garment as he passes by.

> Teach me to do your will for you are my God; may your good spirit lead me on level ground. (Psalm 143:10)

> Be still and know that I am God. (Psalm 46:10)

September 23

Take Responsibility for the Energy You Bring into a room

Oh, that's a good one, huh? Don't you wish you had the nerve to say that to a few people in your past? Or maybe even the present? Whether the energy is positive or negative, if it is strong enough, it will set the tone. Usually, you can feel it instantly. You could cut it with a knife, right? If it's negative, how do you handle it? With compassion? Or do you add fuel to the fire? Most often, those people are having a hard time in their lives. It

may be something they did that caused their attitude or maybe someone else piled a heap of coals on their head. Either way, it's our job to help, whether by a kind word or a simple, silent prayer. God made them and loves them the same as he loves you and me. Even Jesus had a bad day now and then and had to put up with others. We all know what he did. It has something to do with a cheek.

> Be kind and compassionate to one another, forgiving each other, just as in Christ God forgave you. (Ephesians 4:32)

September 24

A Man Reaps What He Sows

This verse, Galatians 6:7, actually pertains to the family of believers. We have such a vast cloud of people around us who we can depend on to reach out to us in our time of need. It works both ways. We can consider one another a blessing from God. It goes back to the Golden Rule. Did you know that was conceived in the Bible? "Do unto others as you would have them do unto you" (Matthew 7:12). Jesus preached it constantly.

> Carry each other's burdens and in this way you will fulfill the law of God. (Galatians 6:2)

> Let us not become weary in doing good, for at the proper time we will reap a harvest if we will not give up. Therefore, as we have opportunity, let us do good to all people, especially to those who belong to the family of believers. (Galatians 6:9–10)

September 25

Decide from Right or Wrong, Not Emotions

Emotions can keep us in bondage. Satan loves to hit on our emotions and wants to jump on and ride the roller coaster of our minds. However, we can take total control over him because God has given us the authority to do so. If you desire to be in God's will and are living a life that glorifies

him, you can be assured he will help you make the right decisions. Keep moving forward until a door is closed. At that time, ask for direction again. His compass never fails. It always leads to Victory Lane. But remember, God's victory may look different from ours. But it is a victory nonetheless.

> With God we will gain the victory and he will trample down our enemies. (Psalm 60:12)

> But thanks be to God; He gives us the victory through our Lord Jesus Christ. (1 Corinthians 15:57)

September 26

Forgiveness for the Sinner

To forgive is to be obedient to God because he commands us to forgive. He doesn't promise that we will forget as he does, but we can renew our soul. If someone we love sins against us, as in unfaithfulness or betrayal, you can be assured that eventually his or her sorrow will be all the punishment he or she will need. The Bible says that we should forgive and comfort that person so he or she will not be overwhelmed with excessive sorrow (2 Corinthians 2:7). It's called sympathy. When we are in the middle of it, not only do we offer comfort for that person but we also comfort and bring peace to ourselves. Unforgiveness is like taking poison yourself and hoping the other person dies.

> For if you forgive men when they sin against you, your heavenly Father will also forgive you. But if you do not forgive others, your Father will not forgive your sins. We are all sinners worthy of grace. (Matthew 6:14)

> If anyone has caused grief, he has not so much grieved me as he has grieved all of you to some extent—not to put it too severely. The punishment inflicted on him by the majority is sufficient. Now instead, you ought to forgive and comfort him, so that he will not be overwhelmed by excessive sorrow. I urge you, therefore, to reaffirm your love for him. Another reason I wrote you was to see if you would stand the test and be obedient in

everything. Anyone you forgive, I also forgive. And what I have forgiven—if there was anything to forgive—I have forgiven in the sight of Christ for your sake, in order that Satan might not outwit us. For we are not unaware of his schemes. (2 Corinthians 2:5–11)

September 27

Jesus Never Changes
God Is Always on His Throne

Isn't that comforting? Psalm 121:7-8 says, "The Lord will keep you from all harm and he will watch over your life. He will watch over your coming and going both now and forever." Have you ever met anyone or had a friend around whom you felt like you were walking on eggshells or thin ice? You never knew if you could just be yourself or not. It's nerve-racking and unsettling, right? I always thought it was just me, but I have come to the conclusion that those people had some tough issues to face. We can count on God to always be the same. We can know there is nothing we can do to lose his love. Take possession of all that God has for you and have no doubt that he's got your back.

Jesus Christ is the same yesterday, today, and forever. (Hebrews 13:9)

No one will be able to stand against you all the days of your life. As I was with Moses, so I will be with you; I will never leave you nor forsake you. (Joshua 1:5)

September 28

Riches

Who do you look to or depend upon for your riches? I'm referring to your pocketbook here. Although we should be seeking spiritual blessings from the Lord as well, more than half of us seek personal riches through the world and ourselves. But what good is it if a man gains the whole world yet forfeits his soul? Or what can anyone give in exchange for his

soul (Matthew 16:26). Many scriptures point to the downfalls of money. Although we need money for obvious reasons, if we don't have God in our lives, money can become the root of all evil. "Seek ye first the kingdom of God [spiritual riches] and all these things [our needs are met] will be given unto you" (Matthew 6:33). Test God and see if this is true.

Do not wear yourself out to get rich; do not trust your own cleverness. (Proverbs 23:4)

If a man will not work, he shall not eat. (2 Thessalonians 3:10)

You can't serve both God and money. (Matthew 6:24)

The love of money is the root of all evil. (1 Timothy 6:10)

Work for the Lord, not for men. (Colossians 3:23)

Moreover, when God gives someone wealth and possessions, and the ability to enjoy them, to accept their lot and be happy in their toil—this is a gift of God. They seldom reflect on the days of their life, because God keeps them occupied with gladness of heart. (Ecclesiastes 5:19-20)

September 29

Mark Your Path before You Begin

When you start out on a long journey, it's best to have some kind of a plan. Otherwise, if you don't know where you're going, how will you know when you've arrived? Let God be your guide. God has an aerial view of your journey. It's like he has already seen a video of your life from beginning to end. If you take Jesus along as your compass, you will eventually get to where you are supposed to be—according to *his* plan, not yours. But it won't necessarily be a smooth ride. You will probably encounter some trouble and setbacks along the way. But if you stick to his path, you can't go wrong. Be guided by his will and his Spirit. It's no fun being lost.

Teach me to do your will; for you are my God; may your good spirit lead me on level ground. (Psalm 143:10)

September 30

Right Facts but Wrong Conclusions

Decisions can be life changing. This makes me ponder human DNA. People being wrongly accused and imprisoned does not just happen in the movies. There are plenty of real-life situations. The prosecutors gathered some facts, questioned a few witnesses, and picked someone who seemed to fit the profile. Is there a worse nightmare than spending years of your life in prison for something you didn't do? What about every-day people, even believers, who condemn their neighbor or a family member simply on a few facts that appear to mark him or her guilty? The facts don't always indicate the truth. Let God be the judge or you may be holding the key to a door that should never have been unlocked.

> The Lord detests lying lips but he delights in men who are truthful. (Proverbs 12:20)

October 1

The Purpose of Prayer: To Communicate With and Hear from God

The story about Jonah is so awesome. You've probably heard how he disobeyed God and then was thrown off a ship and found himself in the belly of a whale. He knew full well that God had put him there. Surprisingly, when Jonah prayed to God he did not ask God to remove him from the whale. Instead, he communicated with God about his disobedience and asked for forgiveness. Even if Jonah had died inside the whale immediately after asking for forgiveness, it would have been better than being released with no response from Jonah regarding what God had asked him to do. Even though Jonah was wrapped in seaweed and was at the bottom of the sea, he knew he needed to talk with God. After Jonah's long and precise prayer, the Lord commanded the fish to vomit

Jonah onto dry land (Jonah 2:10). God gave Jonah deliverance because he chose God's will instead of his own. Sometimes the things we want are not in God's plan for us. He knows what's best and will continue to work in our lives, however painful, to accomplish his purpose. The Lord Jesus taught us to pray for God's will to be done. "Thy will, not mine be done" (Matthew 26:39).

From inside the fish Jonah prayed to the LORD his God. "In my distress I called to the LORD, and he answered me. From deep in the realm of the dead I called for help, and you listened to my cry. You hurled me into the depths, into the very heart of the seas, and the currents swirled about me; all your waves and breakers swept over me. I said, 'I have been banished from your sight; yet I will look again toward your holy temple.' The engulfing waters threatened me, the deep surrounded me; seaweed was wrapped around my head. To the roots of the mountains I sank down; the earth beneath barred me in forever. But you, LORD my God, brought my life up from the pit. "When my life was ebbing away, I remembered you, LORD, and my prayer rose to you, to your holy temple. "Those who cling to worthless idols turn away from God's love for them. But I, with shouts of grateful praise, will sacrifice to you. What I have vowed I will make good. I will say, 'Salvation comes from the LORD.'" And the LORD commanded the fish, and it vomited Jonah onto dry land. (Jonah 2:1-10)

October 2

Defeat the Devil: Love Those He Wants You to Hate

What a great perspective! You'll need God's power to make this happen though, right? This is all about loving the unlovable. We need to look deeper into the souls of those God puts in front of us. You may miss out on a huge blessing if you decide that someone just doesn't appeal to you or isn't your type. I have been put in my place many times. The devil revs up my pride and whispers another lie. He knows the good things God has in store for me, so he tries to steer me in another direction. I once read that there is a storeroom in heaven holding beautifully wrapped boxes containing blessings that God wants to bestow on us. But unfortunately we are never ready to receive them. That seemingly unlovable person may be the key

that opens the door you've been hoping to go through. Ask God how he wants you to handle your situation. He sees it all through a different lens. Remind the devil that he has no power over you.

> In order that Satan might not outwit us. For we are not unaware of his schemes. (2 Corinthians 2:11)

> Put on the full armor of God, so that you can take your stand against the devil's schemes. (Ephesians 6:11)

October 3

Go Even When You Don't Feel Like Going

God has promised to see you through all of your trials. He may not take them away, but he will go through them with you, hand in hand. At one point, Paul headed into a dangerous, life-threatening storm through obedience to God. Paul felt that it wasn't necessary for him to live but it was necessary for him to go. No one has ever gone through a trial without coming out the other side a better person. God allows his children to go through hard times because perseverance produces the character he desires to see in you. Paul was not only blessed for his obedience but he also passed those blessings onto others. Sometimes God calms the storm; sometimes he calms the child.

> Blessed is the man who perseveres under trial because when he has stood the test he will receive the crown of life that God has promised to those who love him. (James 1:12)

> Let us run with perseverance, the race marked out for us. (Hebrews 12:1)

October 4

Love and Value Yourself; God Has
Invested a Great Deal in You

Before you can love someone else, you need to be able to love yourself. You can't give away something you don't have. You need to know and believe that even if you had been the only person on earth, Jesus would still have gone to the cross for you. You are worth every painful step and breath that Jesus took while carrying that burdensome cross to Calvary. In your humility, you can accept that you are worthy of his love just as you are. You don't have to work at making yourself appear to be loveable to him. He loved you and counted you as worthy even when you were yet in your mother's womb. His handprint was on you before you were born. You are loved, you are valuable, and you are his. Rest in that truth.

Before I formed you in the womb I knew you, before you were born I set you apart. (Jeremiah 1:5)

October 5

Don't Let People Poop in Your Yard

Oftentimes, people will try to make your life miserable just so theirs doesn't look so bad. They act out of revenge, jealousy, or perhaps bitterness. They may believe that old tale about the grass being greener on the other side of the fence. If they can make your yard look bad enough, maybe they won't have to work so hard on their own. Don't let anyone poop in your yard. Don't let anyone drop his or her bundles of insecurity and negativity for you to pick up. Everyone has issues to deal with, and we are not responsible for them. They need to meet God back in their yard and let him mark their boundaries. He will send his rain in due season. Look for it!

A heart at peace gives life to the body, but envy rots the bones. (Proverbs 14:30)

October 6

You Can't Keep Doing the Same Thing and Expect Different Results

Have you ever watched someone keep doing the same thing over and over again and not understand why things didn't change? He or she thinks they are victims. They expect God or someone else to jump in and change things. If our efforts are not producing fruit, maybe we need a little pruning. Sometimes we need to be willing to take a serious look at ourselves and be ready to go under the shears. Perhaps we are seeking a result with the wrong motive. If we are seeking to please ourselves, we will find that our arrogance will get us nowhere. We get what we sow, and if we keep using the same dull needle, we lose our battle. Make your plans and decisions on the basis of your relationship with God, not on how you feel. Emotions can sometimes get in your way.

> You do not have because you do not ask God. When you ask, you do not receive because you ask with the wrong motives, that you may spend what you get on your pleasures. (James 4:3)

October 7

Don't Compromise Your Faith to Meet Your Desires

Don't sit on the fence, don't be the color gray, and don't say no when you should say yes. Pray for spiritual strength, and make the Holy Spirit your guide. Be on your guard, and stand firm in your faith. Set an example for other believers in love and stand up for Jesus and his truths. Be God's hands and feet. Make your desires his desires, and watch your life and doctrine closely. Persevere in both because if you do, you will save yourself and be a soul-winner for God. Plant the seed and let the Holy Spirit do the watering.

> Be on your guard; stand firm in your faith; be men of courage; be strong. Do everything in love. (1 Corinthians 16:13–14)

Watch your life and doctrine closely. Persevere in them, because if you do, you will save both yourself and your hearers. (1 Timothy 4:16)

October 8

Give Satan a Bad Day

How do you think Satan would describe a bad day for himself? If you turn the other cheek? If you let someone have that parking spot close to the door? If you volunteer even with a busy schedule? Maybe if you say yes when you'd rather say no? Or how about if you turn down a fun night out to stay home and have personal time with Jesus? What would Satan do if you shared Jesus with the checkout person? What would happen if you did all of these things in a single day? I think we could surely chalk that up as a bad day for Satan. If he "prowls around like a roaring lion looking for someone to devour" (1 Peter 5:8), he probably won't find you. As a matter of fact, he probably won't bother with you for a good while. He knows whose you are and that he can't compete! Be the kind of person that when your feet first touch the floor in the morning, Satan says, "Oh crap, she's up!"

October 9

Be the Best You Can Possibly Be—for Jesus' Sake

Have you ever thought about how Paul delighted in being somewhat of a slave to everyone to win as many as possible for the Lord? He was some guy, huh? He was definitely someone I would not or could not compare myself to. He was a true soul-winner for Jesus' sake. That's what he set out to be. In our little corner of the world it seems different. Unlike Paul, we live in a busy and time-consuming world with family, friends, work, and life using up most of our day. So we need to create quality rather than quantity time with the Creator. Discipline yourself to get up ten minutes earlier than usual to start your day with God. Be the best you can possibly be—for Jesus' sake.

Go into all the world and preach the good news to all creation. (Mark 16:15)

To the weak I became weak, to win the weak. I have become all things to all people so that by all possible means I might save some. I do all this for the sake of the gospel that I may share in its blessings. (1 Corinthians 9:22-23)

October 10

Everyone Has Twenty-Four Hours in a Day

God made the day and gave it to us. If we are children of the King, we can experience God twenty-four hours a day, even though we walk in a carnal world. He never forces himself on us. He gives us free will, and so we can choose whether or not to give some part of our day back to him, whether it is five minutes while showering or fifteen minutes during our drive to work or an evening Bible study. Going to church once a week usually doesn't manifest all we need of God. He made us to need him. He made us with a hole in our heart that only he can fill. Seek him often, open the door, and you will find him. The hole in your heart will be filled 24–7!

Ask and it will be given to you; seek and you will find; knock and the door will be opened unto you. (Matthew 7:7)

Here I am! I stand at the door and knock. If anyone hears my voice and opens the door, I will come in and eat with that person, and they with me. (Revelation 3:20)

October 11

Wine Is a Mocker and Beer a Brawler

Moderation is a great practice in all walks of life. Too much of anything is not always good; more is not necessarily better. Whether a social drinker, a lone drinker, or someone who doesn't engage at all, we all know the downfall of those who drink too much. And the ripple effect is staggering

to their loved ones. If you have someone in your life who has had problems with alcohol and it has poisoned your walk, you know far too well what I'm talking about. Altering your mood usually puts you on a new path—a different way of discernment or possibly no discernment at all. It's a slippery slope, and you may not know you're on the way down until you hit the bottom. The way back up is a much more difficult climb. Ask God to set you free from any addiction. His grace will be sufficient for you. (2Corinthians 12:9)

Set me free from my prison that I may praise your holy name. (Psalm 142:7)

Teach me to do your will, for you are my God; may your good Spirit lead me on level ground. (Psalm 143:10)

October 12

"Avoid a Man Who Talks Too Much"
(Proverbs 29:19)

A man who talks too much is usually either running someone down or exalting himself. He likes stirring up dissension by betraying a confidence or stretching the truth. He usually is a person with low self-esteem and lacks confidence so he runs someone else down to make himself look good. I think that's called arrogance, right? He's the one sitting at a table next to an empty chair when a group gathers. Who needs it, right? Aren't we all looking for encouragement and validation? A wise man or woman with a quiet, gentle spirit speaks from his or her heart, and you will be wise to surround yourself with people of that demeanor. But in the meantime, say a little prayer for the person next to the empty chair.

You brood of vipers, how can you who are evil say anything good? For the mouth speaks what the heart is full of. (Matthew 12:34)

October 13

The Unforgivable Sin:
Blasphemy against the Holy Spirit

Those who blaspheme the Holy Spirit are those who consciously and perhaps repeatedly reject Jesus Christ as their Lord and Savior and are not even concerned about it. Blasphemy is an act of contempt, insult, and a lack of reverence for God. It is the continual state of unbelief and the only unforgivable sin. God's undeniable will for you is to be filled with the Holy Spirit (Ephesians 5:15–18).

In John 3:16–21, Jesus says over and over that whoever believes in him will have eternal life and that whoever does not believe stands condemned already. Man rejects God in fear that man's evil deeds will be exposed, and sometimes pride gets in the way. Jesus charges a person with blasphemy because he sees that his or her heart is hard and determined to reject him, and that he or she will never repent. God is just and will not forgive this sin. If you haven't believed and accepted God's free gift of Jesus, you won't one day walk the streets of gold. On judgment day, God will say to those unbelievers, "I never knew you" (Matthew 7:23). If you know someone who is in continual unbelief, show them the following scriptures. That person will thank you for your boldness and for saving their soul. And they will be forgiven.

> Whoever blasphemes against the Holy Spirit will never be forgiven; he is guilty of an eternal sin. (Mark 3:29)

> And everyone who speaks a word against the Son of Man will be forgiven, but anyone who blasphemes against the Holy Spirit will not be forgiven. (Luke 12:10)

> And so I tell you, every kind of sin and slander can be forgiven, but blasphemy against the Spirit will not be forgiven. (Matthew 12:31)

October 14

Sorrow without Despair
Reveals Us to Ourselves

Despair steals the truth from us. When we are in despair, nothing makes sense. Sorrow without despair, however, reveals a lot. Sorrow is a deep emotion with great power to show us what God really wants us to know. God uses it for our good. Through sorrow, God shows us what we're really made of, and we see ourselves as he does. We enter into the deep chamber of our soul and become closer to God. We see what he sees, hear what he hears, and become the light in the world he predestined us to be. Godly sorrow will eventually bring you joy.

> Godly sorrow brings repentance that leads to salvation and leaves no regret, but worldly sorrow brings death [spiritual death]. (2 Corinthians 7:10)

October 15

You Are Redeemed, Justified, and Set Free

Redeemed: saved by Jesus because he paid the debt for our sins
Justified: found not guilty
Free: no bounty on our head

Did you ever have a revelation that made you think, *Wow, this is what it means to be free!* Maybe after you paid off a high credit card balance or after you served time in jail or prison? How about college graduation or retirement? Because Jesus found you guiltless and paid your debt, thus removing the bounty on your head, you are redeemed, justified, and free! How does that feel? Don't think for a minute that you're not worthy of God's gift. Jesus didn't die for *some* people; he died for *all* people. Don't think you have to clean yourself up before he can free you. He takes you just as you are. His spilled blood is the cloth that cleanses you. It's not a visible cloth; you must see it by faith. He loves you so much that he gave his own life so you could spend eternity with him. That's freedom!

In him we have redemption through his blood and the forgiveness of sins in accordance with riches of God's grace that he lavished on us with all wisdom and understanding. (Ephesians 1:7)

All the prophets testify about him that everyone who believes in him receives forgiveness of sins through his name. (Acts 10:43)

October 16

Fragrant Forgiveness

God's forgiveness is like a fragrant, soothing ointment. True forgiveness is hard to describe. Many people in the world forgive but not many forget. God says in the book of Isaiah that he blots out our sins and remembers them no more (Isaiah 43:25). We can say, "Lord, I'm so sorry for that particular sin," and he will answer, "What sin?" When we ask for his sweet forgiveness and repent and ask him to be in our lives, our slates are wiped clean with that invisible cloth. The fragrance of his forgiveness lingers. Bathe in it.

Jesus said, "Father, forgive them for they know not what they do." (Luke 23:34)

But you are a forgiving God, gracious and compassionate, slow to anger and abounding in love. (Nehemiah 9:17)

October 17

Overcoming

Do you have someone in your life who likes to push your buttons? Is it a child, parent, family member, or maybe spouse? It will most likely be someone you actually love. It will be easier to keep yourself under control than to try to change the other person. You can only be responsible for yourself. You overcome your weaknesses by taking on God's strengths. Our human nature is so easily aroused, but if we put on the mind of Christ, we can overcome. Pray "Lord, change me," not "Lord, change him or her."

If we believe the other person needs to change, we are blaming them for our feelings. It's not about anyone else; it's about us. If we allow God to renew our minds, we will see the other person and the circumstances from a whole new perspective.

Don't think you can do it alone or hope the other person will make the first move. Let God do it for you. Then give him the glory.

> Do not conform to the pattern of this world, but be transformed by the renewing of your mind. (Romans 12:2)

> For the foolishness of God is wiser than man's wisdom, and the weakness of God is stronger that man's strength. (1 Corinthians 1:25)

October 18

"Job Went through All of his Trials without Charging God with Any Wrongdoing"
(Job 1:22)

The Bible is not about Job or Isaiah or Paul. Every book is about God. It's all about him! The story of Job and the others were written to help us through our daily lives. We are supposed to learn something from every story. To read and walk away mystified is to have read in vain. The gospel parables are examples and analogies of what we may go through in this life and prepare us for the next. If we find ourselves in a trial, we need to persevere and come out the other side a new and better person. Don't ask God why. Rather, ask, "Why not?" Job never charged God with any wrongdoing. He held on tight to God's hand simply because he knew it was better to walk in the dark with his God than in the light without him.

> Woe to him who quarrels with his Maker, to him who is but a potsherd [broken pottery] among the potsherds on the ground. (Isaiah 45:9)

> For it is better, if it is God's will, to suffer for doing good than for doing evil. (1Peter 3:17)

Dear friends, do not be surprised at the fiery ordeal that has come on you to test you, as though something strange were happening to you. But rejoice inasmuch as you participate in the sufferings of Christ, so that you may be overjoyed when his glory is revealed. (1Peter 4:12-13)

He took a piece of broken pottery and scraped himself ... Job said, "Shall we accept good things from God and not trouble?" (Job 2:8, 10)

October 19

Sometimes God Allows Sickness or Trials so Jesus Will be Glorified

Mary and Martha loved their brother Lazarus, who was deathly ill. They summoned Jesus to come because they knew he felt the same about Lazarus and could heal him. But disappointment set in when Jesus tarried and Lazarus breathed his last. Mary and Martha were distraught and hurt because Jesus didn't come in time. Jesus told his disciples, "Lazarus has fallen asleep; but I am going there to wake him up" (John 11:11). Jesus was speaking of death, but his disciples thought he meant natural sleep. Lazarus had been dead four days by the time Jesus arrived. Jesus purposely waited to perform the miracle of calling Lazarus back to life so the disciples would see and believe. When God doesn't answer your prayers immediately, know that he is in the process of working things out for his glory. Miracles don't just happen; all things need to be in alliance with God's perfect plan. Don't pick your mercies green!

In this you will rejoice, though now for a little while you may have had to suffer grief in all kinds of trials. These have come so that your faith—of greater worth than gold, which perishes even though refined by fire—may be proved genuine and may result in praise, glory and honor when Jesus Christ is revealed. (1 Peter 1:6–7)

Read John 11:1–45.

October 20

The New Testament:
Culmination of Old Testament Prophecies

When I was a new Christian at twenty-five, I seldom found interest in the Old Testament. During my study of the New Testament, however, I was amazed how they interacted and that the prophecies of the Old Testament were fulfilled in the New Testament.

Many skeptics say that mere man compiled the Bible and that it has changed often over the years. Rightly so, it did change and man did write the Bible, but with total inspiration from God. He gave us this book strictly for our benefit of knowing him and understanding how to live our lives. Second Timothy 3:16–17 states, "All scripture is God-breathed and is useful for teaching, rebuking, correcting and training in righteousness so that the man of God may be thoroughly equipped for every good work." God would never have allowed his words to say something other than what he wants us to know. God has control over man, not the other way around. The Old Testament prophecies reaching fruition in the New Testament is so phenomenal. No mere man could ever have made it up. So if you're looking for a faith builder, know that God's book may have become easier to understand over the years but has never altered from the truth God speaks to us today in the New Testament. Remember, too, that the Old Testament was under the law but the New Testament is because of Jesus. We are no longer under the old law.

October 21

Losing Sight of the Gift Giver

Usually gifts are given out of love, whether they are monetary or spiritual. There is always a message, spoken or silent, from the giver. If we think too much of the gift, we may miss the heart and generosity of the giver. When God sends us a blessing, he wants us to notice him. If we enjoy the gift too much and it becomes an idol, we may lose our focus on where it came from. God is a jealous God (Exodus 20:5). If you lose sight of him, seek

him with all your heart and soul and you will find him once again. This is what God desires from you. Then you will truly know and love the Giver.

> For the Lord your God is a consuming fire; a jealous God. (Deuteronomy 4:24)

October 22

The Proverbs 31 Woman

No woman, married or single, dares to compare herself to the Proverbs 31 woman! It would be good to strive for these attributes, but please know that God loves and accepts you just the way you are. In God's eyes, you come very close to the woman described in Proverbs. Solomon was generally credited for a large portion of the book, but it is believed to be inspired by God. It is a book filled with wisdom. If you're a woman and have a desire to please the Lord, soak in the knowledge and wisdom God has provided in Proverbs. You'll most likely come across a few rubies along the way.

> Many women do noble things but you surpass them all. (Proverbs 31:29)

> The wife of noble character who can find? She is worth far more than rubies. (Proverbs 31:10)

October 23

Remember Where Your Power Source Lies

One of the things God hates most is pride. Pride goes before destruction. Realizing that your strength comes from God is a step in the right direction, and you need look nowhere else. You will continually stumble through life if you put yourself on the pedestal instead of God. You can be crazy busy, whether for yourself or for God, but if you exalt yourself, what good comes of it? God gives us each day, and he is the one who gives us breath. Be exhausted for God, but remember that he is your supply.

As they make music they will sing, "All my fountains are in you." (Psalm 87:7)

But those who hope in the Lord will renew their strength. (Isaiah 40:31)

"Not by might nor by power, but by my Spirit," says the Lord God Almighty. (Zechariah 4:6)

October 24

Hold Up His sheep until They Find God

Like shepherds who watch over their sheep, you can lead the lost to Christ. God calls his sheep by name and will use you to steer them down the right path. Be there for them in love, prayer, and teaching until they are on the level path of God and near the gate. Move them toward the light, and once they reach the outstretched arms of Jesus, they will have eternal life and never be snatched from his grip, never to be lost again.

> Enter through the narrow gate. For wide is the gate and broad is the road that leads to destruction, and many enter through it. But small is the gate and narrow the road that leads to life, and only a few find it. (Matthew 7:13–14)

Jesus said, "Take care of my sheep." (John 21:17)

October 25

Some Things Are Worth Fearing

Consider the following:

- the world taking God out of everything
- greed
- sinning

- backsliding
- not taking God's plan into consideration
- finding security in yourself
- thinking you are in control
- standing opposite from God
- your mind turning on you
- squelching the Holy Spirit
- changing the definition of marriage
- becoming desensitized to abortion

Only God can plunge deep into our soul and make us whole again. We have to bend our knees and say, "God, you alone know, so you alone lead." You can make your own list of fears. Then ask God to turn the light on in your soul.

October 26

"A Household Divided against Itself Cannot Stand"
(Matthew 3:25)

We can use the word *household* as a synonym for church, marriage, plans, or family—even politics. To be in agreement is a no-stress situation. To be like-minded is a blessing. To be united is to be strong. To have strength is to be dependent on God. When God is in the midst, all things weak become strong. When a family, marriage, plans, or church have God as its nucleus, it cannot fall. When we have the mind of Christ we know his truths, and those truths will set us free because of the Spirit. Free to be me, free to be you, with Christ in between. United we stand, divided we fall.

> Now the Lord is the Spirit and where the Spirit of the Lord is, there is freedom. (2 Corinthians 3:17)

> A cord of three strands is not easily broken. (Ecclesiastes 4:12)

October 27

People Who Walk in the Spirit
Judge Things, Not People

Aren't you thankful that God doesn't judge you at the end of the day? Yet we judge people around us all day long. God loves the sinner but hates the sin. If we are focused on God, we will see others as he sees them. Instead of judging someone's sin, we can pray for him or her. Constant sin in someone's life indicates they don't know God and they have issues to deal with. They don't see the darkness they are walking in without God and know nothing of the light. Show the lost how to walk in the Spirit by expressing spiritual truths. Once they accept God into their life, they will understand the things that seemed foolish to them in the past.

> There is only one Judge and Lawgiver, the one who is able to save and destroy. But you, who are you to judge your neighbor? (James 4:12)

> You judge by human standards. I pass judgement on no one. (John 8:15)

October 28

Don't Wait to be All Cleaned
Up before Coming to God

Do you understand that Jesus died for you before you were even born? He knew you when you were in your mother's womb, and while you were still a sinner, he died for you. Because Jesus died for you on the cross, you are as cleaned up as you need to be. He invites you to come just as you are. If you wait until you think you are good enough, you'll most likely never accept his invitation. How good would you have to be? When you say you are not worthy, you are saying Jesus' death was not good enough. Don't wait until you feel like you are ready; your salvation comes through faith, not anything you do. It's called grace. Don't allow your past to influence your future.

We believe it is through the grace of our Lord Jesus that we are saved; just as we are. (Acts 15:11)

So if the Son sets you free, you will be free indeed. (John 8:36)

October 29

Live for the Goodness of Others

It is one thing to help someone come out of their sin but yet another to call someone a sinner. It's like the blind leading the blind. When we have a self-oriented agenda, we tend to love ourselves more than anything or anyone else. That is not Christ-like. We are to love our neighbors as ourselves. That is the greatest commandment commissioned by God. It was the first law written on the tablet given to Moses. When you condemn others, it says you don't believe God died for them (John 3:16). Be good and thankful for all the world if for no other reason than to be obedient to God. See them as Christ sees all of us—loved and forgiven by grace. Live for the goodness of others.

> You my brothers were called to be free. But do not use your freedom to indulge the sinful nature; rather serve one another in love. The entire law is summed up in a single command: "Love your neighbor as yourself." (Galatians 5:13–14)

> Therefore, there is now no condemnation for those who are in Christ Jesus because through Christ Jesus the Law of the Spirit of life set me free from the law of sin and death. (Romans 8:1)

October 30

Jesus + Nothing = Salvation

This simple equation pinpoints the whole redemption story. It's about *being* rather than *doing*. It's not about good works, which are the *result* of salvation, not the *cause* of it. The cause of salvation is nothing more than

Jesus. Isn't that comforting? The song "Jesus Paid It All" has a verse that goes like this:

> Jesus paid it all,
> All to Him I owe.
> Sin had left a crimson stain,
> He washed it white as snow.

Christianity is the only religion that allows us to have a personal relationship with our God. Jesus said, "I am the way, the truth and the life—no one comes to the Father but through me" (John 14:6). No more, no less. Just Jesus. If good works could save us, then Jesus died for nothing, right?

> Believe in the Lord Jesus, and you will be saved—you and your household. (Acts 16:31)

> For God so loved the world that he gave his one and only son, that whoever believes in him shall not parish but have eternal life. (John 3:16)

October 31

You Are a Main Character in God's Redemption Story

In the beautiful story of God's redemption, you are no less important than Adam and Eve. When you step onto the stage and act out your life according to God's will, applause rings from heaven. God's plan for you is perfect. He chose you to be his by calling your name. You are redeemed by his willingness to hang on a cross in obedience to his Father. Please don't take this lightly. Redemption is a free gift; all you have to do is accept it. Even if you were the only one on earth, God would still have allowed Jesus' agonizing death. That's how deep and how wide his love is for you. What you do with this life matters. Your life is speaking to you. The stage is quiet, the curtain is up, and the lights are dimmed. Find your place and live it out before the final curtain falls.

In him we have redemption through his blood and the forgiveness of sins; in accordance with the riches of God's grace. (Ephesians 1:7)

November 1

Our Job:
Instruct the Next Generation

Children are God's favorite humans. I think it's because they reflect God's innocence and purity. Children should be taught the concept of God's love. The Bible says to sit by the wayside and tell your children stories of God so they will pass them on to their children and to the following generations. It cannot be an untold story. In God's word, the gospels share the same scripture, "Let the little children come to me. The kingdom of heaven belongs to them." (Matthew 19:14, Mark 10:14, and Luke 18:16). Let your children hear you speaking well of God and his goodness and love. As they grow up with these things in their hearts, they are bound to live them out and pass them on to their children. Each generation will look back and be thankful.

> Listen, my son, to your father's instruction and do not forsake your mother's teaching. They will be a garland to grace your head and a chain to adorn your neck. (Proverbs 1:8–9)

> Train a child in the way he should go, and when he is old he will not turn from it. (Proverbs 22:6)

November 2

The Holy Spirit:
The Basis for Your Confidence

Measure your confidence with the abilities of the Holy Spirit and seek his direction when you are unsure which door to go through. Keep going through the opened doors with faithful courage. The Holy Spirit is like a compass and will help you get to your destination. Letting go of your

own ideas and desires will allow you to trust in God alone. Sometimes we are our own worst enemy. Don't let yourself get in the way. When the Egyptian army was on the trail of the Israelites, the Red Sea did not part for the Israelites until their toes touched the water. God wanted them to trust in him, not themselves. They knew they had to get to the other side and trusted in God to make it happen. With confidence in the Holy Spirit's leading, they made it to the other side just before God allowed the waters to roll over the army. It's quite a story in Exodus 14. Read it!

Be still and know that I am God. (Psalm 46:10)

Teach me to do your will for you are my God; may your good spirit lead me on level ground. (Psalm 143:10)

November 3

Stuck in God's Waiting Room?
You Are Not Alone

The Old Testament is full of examples of God's people waiting for him to move. God's waiting room is much larger and busier than any doctor's office. Like a baby waiting to be born, God wants to get you in the perfect position. As hard as that anxious mother may push, the birth won't happen until that baby is in the correct position. And just like that baby, God won't use you until you are ready. Like Joseph, Abraham, and Moses waited on God, we must wait patiently. Delay does not mean denial. Trust that God will move when the time and conditions are right. Even Jesus had to wait thirty years until all the prophecies, plans, and people were in place. Do not be anxious, but let God lead you in his perfect way. Don't pick your mercies green.

Wait on the Lord; be strong and take heart and wait on the Lord. (Psalm 27:14)

November 4

Hang on to the Coattails of Jesus

As I thought of this phrase, I pictured Jesus' coattails being ripped to shreds as people of every age clung tightly to him as he walked along and touched them with his mighty power. When our world turns crazy and seems to be coming apart at the seams, let's remember that the shredded fabric is just a touch away. Like the woman in the Bible who was healed just by touching Jesus' garment as he walked by (Mark 5:27-29), we have the same mercy and grace that was granted to her. She was healed because she believed that Jesus could and would do it. His garment is strong and durable and will never shrink or shred. Seek him above all else, and he will be there for you. No storm is ever outside the reach of Jesus' robe!

> People brought all their sick to him and begged him to let the sick just touch the edge of his robe and all who touched him were healed. (Matthew 14:36)

November 5

Satan Destroys Relationships

Be alert to Satan's schemes. He uses the tiniest, insignificant things to cause trouble between God's people as well as the following:

- unkindness
- preoccupation
- defensiveness
- nagging
- sarcasm
- criticism
- ingratitude
- boredom
- jealousy
- envy
- greed

- selfishness
- neglecting the Lord's house

Resist Satan and stand firm in your faith. Remember, "Satan himself masquerades as an angel of light" (2 Corinthians 11:14). But God has given us total authority over him. Tell Satan you're a child of God and in the name of Jesus he must go.

Resist the devil and He will set you free. (James 4:7)

Be self-controlled and alert. Your enemy, the devil prowls around like a hungry lion looking for someone to devour. (1 Peter 5:8–9)

November 6

Don't Let Your Attitude Keep You from Your Destiny

Bad attitudes stink, right? Like dead fish left on the shore to rot. Have you ever gotten up on the wrong side of the bed and then all day you blame everyone you run into for your bad day? I think attitude, like happiness or forgiveness, is a choice. Usually, a bad attitude is because we are not right with God. It could be a signal that your connection with God is broken or short-circuited, so to speak. You are the only one who can fix that. Not even God can do it. He beckons, but it comes back to choice again—your choice. Try talking with him the first thing in the morning before you get out of bed and before you face anyone else. First, thank him for another day, and then ask him to guard your thoughts and your heart as you go out into the world. Your new attitude could cause a big change in your day. It's your choice. Be destined for a good day. Let God put a new song in your mouth!

May the words of my mouth and the meditation of my heart be pleasing in your sight, O Lord, my Rock and my Redeemer. (Psalm 19:14)

Out of the overflow of the heart, the mouth speaks. (Matthew 12:34)

November 7

Everyone Has Something to Give Away

I hope you have experienced how a boomerang works so you can understand this concept. You toss it away and it ends up coming right back. I believe that's also God's concept of "doing to others what you would have them do unto you" (Luke 6:31). Whether it's money, forgiveness, happiness, help, knowledge, wisdom, love, kindness, support, life, grace, mercy, or time, when you give it away, it will come back threefold.

God loved us first and hoped we would love him back. That was his only purpose in creating us. So to not love him is to not fulfill our purpose, right? His greatest commandment was to share our love, to give it away freely as he did, without conditions. He says we must seek him. When we do that and make him the center of our lives, he fills our every need. Seek him, find him, and then give him to someone else!

Freely you have received, freely give. (Matthew 10:8)

November 8

"A Prudent Wife Is from the Lord"
(Proverbs 19:14)

Prudent: cautious, managing very carefully, discreet, tactful, modest ...

Proverbs is a favorite book of many believers. It talks to all types of people: young and old, male and female, rich and poor, married or single. Your Bible concordance will list all the scriptures that pertain to a prudent wife. Some great ones are in Proverbs, but there are many throughout both the Old and New Testament.

A quarrelsome wife is like a constant dripping. (Proverbs 19:13)

A wife of noble character. (Proverbs 12:4)

The husband must love his wife as he loves himself. (Ephesians 5:33)

Read Proverbs 31:10–31 for a biblical description of a wife of noble character.

November 9

In His Presence

Our God is the one true God, and he tells us all throughout the Bible to continue to walk in the light of his presence. That means being so right with God that we are in the immediate area that surrounds him. We cannot flee from his presence. We are so near to him, we can feel the brush of his robe when he passes by. This is awesome! Let this truth soak into your heart and soul. This is his will. Choose it for yourself, and give it to others. You can choose him or let the darkness of the world consume you. Know the truth and the truth will set you free (John 8:32).

> When Jesus spoke to the people, he said, "I am the light of the world. Whoever follows me will never walk in darkness but will have the light of life." (John 8:12)

November 10

Get Rid of the Backpack

What do you carry in your backpack? Everyone has one and some are a little heavier than others. Some carry selfish decisions along with unforgiveness, greed, hate, mistrust, self-loathing, unbelief, laziness, jealousy, sinfulness, doubt, defensiveness, pride, manipulation, and so on. Any of these sound familiar? How long and how far have you carried these things? Isn't it time to put them down? These items are not from God. Nor are they his will for you. Make a decision today to let go of that heavy burden. Replace the backpack with a basket filled with the fruit of the Holy Spirit: love, joy, peace, patience, kindness, goodness, faithfulness, gentleness, and self-control. The backpack will be easier to carry and bottomless. At any

time, you can reach inside and take out whatever you need. It will be a life-changer and no longer a back-breaker.

> But the fruit of the Spirit is love, joy, peace, patience, kindness, goodness, faithfulness, gentleness, and self-control. (Galatians 5:22)

November 11

You Don't Need More Faith, Just More Faithfulness

Faith is a noun. It's something we possess. *Faithfulness* describes how we handle our faith. It's like knowledge and wisdom; knowledge is a noun, something we possess, while wisdom describes how we use that knowledge. If you don't have both, one is no good without the other. Faith is something God gives us, and our faithfulness is what we give back to him. It is being loyal, constant, unwavering, devoted, and true. It's like having a lifesaver thrown to you in the water and thankfully grabbing hold of it to survive. In Luke you can read the story about the sinful woman who washed Jesus' feet with her tears because of her faithfulness (Luke 7:37-38). You already have the faith; it's what you do with it that counts.

> Now faith is confidence in what we hope for and assurance about what we do not see. (Hebrews 11:1)

November 12

"Church Didn't Do Anything for Me"

This is a common response to an invite to church. It just makes you wonder: Did they go for themselves or to find God? You alone need to meet God face-to-face. If you haven't lifted the veil from your face, you haven't seen him clearly. Nor have you received his full radiance. For whatever reason you haven't found a church that suits you, give God another try. Ask him to show you which church he wants you in. Visit a

few, and let faith lead you to discover who God really is. He is waiting to see you unveiled. Only in Christ is the veil taken away.

> But whenever anyone turns to the Lord, the veil is taken away. (2 Corinthians 3:16–17)

November 13

Don't Just Pray

Even though God says you do not have because you do not ask (James 4:2), it doesn't mean you can sit and do nothing after submitting your requests. Many Old Testament people worked hard and had to persevere through much hardship after asking God for help. God comes to our aid sometimes through very unusual circumstances. Stay alert and sensitive to the moving of the Holy Spirit. Even though it doesn't appear to be the right way, if God opens the door, go through it. If he closes it, look for an open window. God's people usually take the narrow road and the one less traveled.

> Being confident of this; that he who began a good work in you will carry it on to completion until the day of Christ Jesus. (Philippians 1:6)

> In his heart a man plans his course, but the Lord determines his steps. (Proverbs 16:9)

> Be still and know that I am God. (Psalm 46:10)

November 14

Have Confidence That Nothing Is Larger Than God

God is large enough for the whole world to rest in his shadow. He is always the bigger, better choice. Since God is faithful to his promises, you can

count on him to take care of anything you bring to his table. He created the moon, the sun, the day, the night, the water, the land and everything in the world and eventually he created *you* and said it was *all good*.

He hovers over us. (Psalm 91:1)

Persevere and you will receive what he has promised. (Hebrews 10:35–36)

He will keep your foot from being snared. (Proverbs 3:26)

God is the one who allows the clouds to drop the dew. (Proverbs 3:20)

And no one gets to Him but through Jesus. (John 14:6)

November 15

Let Wisdom Dictate Your Friendships

Friendships are a gift and blessing from God. He uses them to aid us in life. Some are short, teaching us a particular thing God wants us to know and then dissolve without a care, while others are longer lasting and serve a larger purpose. Always ask yourself, "Where is God in this relationship?" Ask God to give you knowledge and wisdom regarding it. Will it bring about good? Strength? Is the other person serving God? Does the friendship cause your faith to grow? Does it bring value and purpose to your life?

Remember, the Bible says we are to be equally yoked (2Corinthians 6:14). Whether it's long or short term, a friendship outside of God's will can cause a lifetime of heartache. Do you need to let go of a friendship or maybe change the boundaries within that relationship? Proverbs is all about wisdom. Proverbs 4:9 says, "She will set a garland of grace on your head and present you with a crown of splendor." Wisdom should be guarded at all costs because it is your life. God gave us wisdom; we should use it.

Make level paths for your feet and take only ways that are firm. (Proverbs 4:26)

November 16

God Sees You as a Beautiful Jewel

In season twelve of *American Idol*, a contestant sang *I Am Beautiful*. One of the stanzas reads,

> He says I'm beautiful
> and I'm worth every tear and every scar.
> And even when you say I'm not
> He says I'm beautiful.

Don't ever judge yourself against someone else's beauty, inside or out. God made and blessed you to be uniquely you. I'm not saying any of us are flawless; only Jesus is flawless and without sin. But it's because of Jesus that God sees us as righteous. Jesus paid a huge price for our beauty, and our gentle and quiet spirit is of great worth to God. Don't seek to find beauty in your appearance with expensive clothes and jewelry. God searches the hearts of his people and will make you his own based on that fact alone.

> Your beauty should not come from outward adornment, such as elaborate hairstyles and the wearing of gold jewelry or fine clothes. Rather, it should be that of your inner self, the unfading beauty of a gentle and quiet spirit, which is of great worth in God's sight. (Peter 3:3–4)

November 17

Be on Your knees for Strength to Stand before the Enemy

Do you have a particular weapon you use to fight off the enemy when he shows up at your door? Ephesians 10 refers to putting on the full armor of

God to take your stand against the devil's schemes. Don't fool yourself—to be a true Christian soldier, you must have God as your commander. He knows every evil and sly trick the devil can devise. Scripture is your ammunition just as Jesus quoted scripture when he was tempted by Satan in the desert. When you praise God out loud and use his word against Satan he will most likely leave you alone. The bible says we have total authority over him (Luke 10:19). That's God speaking, so when the enemy trespasses on your domain, pull out your weapons of power and praise and send God to answer the door. The victory will be yours. And you will be left standing.

> Submit yourselves, then, to God. Resist the devil, and he will flee from you. (James 4:7)

November 18

"If I Have Not Love, I Am Nothing"
(1Corinthians 13:2)

Paul was preaching to the believers in Corinth, explaining the meaning and power of love and what it looks like. First Corinthians 13 is all about God's gift of love, and it ends, saying, "Faith, hope, and love; the greatest of these is love" (1Corinthians 13:13). We need to move love from the brain to the heart. Just like salvation, that's the only way to understand its meaning and effect. Both salvation and love come from God, and without them we have nothing. God showed us what love looks like by sending his Son, Jesus, to die on the cross for our sins. It is an example of how we are to love one another: pure, sweet, unconditional love. Without God you cannot know true love, and without true love you cannot be all that he has planned for you to be.

> Dear friends, let us love one another, for love comes from God. Everyone who loves has been born of God and knows God. Whoever does not love does not know God, because God is love. This is how God showed his love among us: He sent his one and only Son into the world that we might live through him. This is love: not that we loved God, but that he loved us and sent his Son as an atoning sacrifice for our sins. Dear friends, since God

so loved us, we also ought to love one another. No one has ever seen God; but if we love one another, God lives in us and his love is made complete in us. (John 4:7–12)

Read 1 Corinthians 13.

November 19

You can be a Part of How Your Story Ends

What story do you want your life to tell? How do you want to be remembered? Don't let anyone else decide that for you. You are a unique individual and so your story should be. As you find your true potential and proceed on your journey toward God, it will all work out according to his plan. God actually knows your story because he wrote it before you were ever born. In his eyes, it is perfect from beginning to end. If we seek God's will for our lives, every line and every chapter will be a journey of his making. The only part of our lives that God does not control is our free will. Our decisions along the way will either make or break our stride. Stay on the straight and narrow. Get out of the way and let God lead. And when you reach his open arms at the end of the journey, he will say, "Well done, good and faithful servant. Well done!" (Matthew 25:23).

> I have fought the good fight, I have finished the race; I have kept the faith. (2 Timothy 4:7)

> For you created my inmost being; you knit me together in my mother's womb. I praise you because I am fearfully and wonderfully made; your works are wonderful, I know that full well. My frame was not hidden from you when I was made in the secret place, when I was woven together in the depths of the earth. Your eyes saw my unformed body; all the days ordained for me were written in your book before one of them came to be. (Psalm 139:13–16)

November 20

"He Who Watches over You
Will Not Slumber"
(Psalm 121:3)

At those low points in our lives when we feel like we've been left alone to fight for ourselves, it seems as though God is nowhere to be found. All throughout the Bible are scriptures that assure us of God's everlasting love and presence. Psalm 121:3 says he will neither slumber nor sleep and that he will watch over our coming and going both now and forever! Doesn't that give you a secure, peaceful feeling? Who or what else should we fear? Even when we are in the dark holding God's hand, it is better than walking in the light without him. Seek him first thing in the morning and he will be with you all throughout the day and into the night. Sleep well!

> I will lie down and sleep in peace, for you alone, O Lord, make me dwell in safety. (Psalm 4:8)

November 21

"To Whom Much Is Given
Much Is Required"
(Luke 12:48)

Many stories in the Bible remind us of God's generosity to us and what he expects from us in return.

Forgiveness
"Forgive and you shall be forgiven" (Luke 6:38).

Merciful
"Be merciful just as your Father is merciful" (Luke 6:36).
"Blessed are those who are merciful for they shall be shown mercy" (Matthew 5:7).

Generous
"Freely you have received, freely give" (Matthew 10:8).

Love
"Love your enemies and pray for those who persecute you" (Matthew 5:44).

Truth
"Know the truth and the truth will set you free" (John 8:32).
"He delights in men who are truthful" (Proverbs 12:22).

Teach
"You call me teacher ... I have set you an example that you should do as I have done for you" (John 13:12, 17).

November 22

Actions Speak Louder Than Words

Jesus was our best example of how to respond to this world we live in. Even though he wasn't short on words, his actions and love are what brought him to his death. He did so willingly. His words were loud only because they made perfect sense and people would hover around him to listen to his gentle teaching. As he carried his cross to Golgotha, he never uttered a word until just before he died. He said, "Father, forgive them for they know not what they are doing" (Luke 23:34). Then, as his last act on earth, he died and saved the world.

> What good is it, my brothers and sisters, if someone claims to have faith but has no deeds? Can such faith save them? Suppose a brother or a sister is without clothes and daily food. If one of you says to them, "Go in peace; keep warm and well fed," but does nothing about their physical needs, what good is it? (James 2:14–16)

November 23

Our Children can Inherit God's Promises or take on our Fears

God never changes; he's the same yesterday, today, and tomorrow. That means the promises he made from the very beginning of time can never change because he sealed them with his own blood. They are for all those who believe, and they will last throughout eternity. God tells us to pass on his promises to all generations. He wants us to teach our children to look for his blessings and to share his promises with them and with their children so they will be passed from generation to generation. His promises far outweigh anything we fear. Human fear arises only when we put ourselves in charge. The only good fear is a high reverence for God. His promises are real, and you can trust he will stand behind them. Be obedient, love and serve the Lord, and he will give you the desires of your heart.

> Blessed is she who has believed that what the Lord has said to her will be accomplished. (Luke 1:45)

> His mercy extends to those who fear him, from generation to generation. (Luke 1:50)

> Do not fear for I am with you; do not be dismayed for I am your God. (Isaiah 41:10)

> Teach them to your children, talking about them when you sit at home and when you walk along the road, when you lie down and when you get up. (Deuteronomy 11:19)

November 24

Don't Exchange the Truth of God for a Lie

It seems that many of God's chosen are spiritually blind. They are not willing to give up the life they are now living for the life God has planned for them. They exchange the truth of God for Satan's lie. The Bible

says Satan is the father of all lies (John 8:4). Many deeds are done in disobedience to our heavenly Father, and in doing so he is dishonored. If you say you believe in God, why do you act as though he doesn't exist? Good question! Don't compromise your faith. When Satan knocks at your door, send Jesus to answer it.

> Your enemy the devil prowls around like a roaring lion looking for someone to devour. (1 Peter 5:8)

> I am the way, the truth and the life. No one comes to the Father but through me. (John 14:6)

> Know the truth and the truth will set you free. (John 8:32)

November 25

The Way Things Are May Not Be the Way They Are Supposed to Be

Have you ever come to the conclusion that maybe you are way off track, maybe out on a limb that can't hold your weight? Did you get in that situation because you took your focus off Jesus like Peter did when he was walking toward him on the water? Peter looked at his own fear and started to sink (Matthew 14:25–33), but Jesus reached out his hand and caught him. Proverbs 15:21–22 tells us that many times our own folly and lack of judgment is our downfall. God has a different perspective about almost everything. He sees a completely different view from what we see through our rose-colored glasses. Ask him to keep you on solid ground and the right path: *his* path. And take off those silly glasses!

> Trust in the Lord with all your heart and lean not on your own understanding; in all your ways acknowledge him, and he will make your paths straight. (Proverbs 3:5–6)

> Folly delights a man who lacks judgment, but a man of understanding keeps a straight course. (Proverbs 3:21)

Show me your ways, O Lord, teach me your paths; guide me in your truth and teach me, for you are God my Savior, and my hope is in you all day long. (Psalm 25:4–5)

November 26

Be the Solution, Not the Problem

In order to be a solution, you must first seek the Lord's wisdom. Wisdom is knowing what to do with the knowledge you have been given. They are both gifts to pass on to be a solution to someone else's problem. God sets these relationships up. It may be for a day, a month, a year, or a lifetime. But remember, its God's wisdom, not your own thoughts or opinions. You need to ask for guidance and direction from the Holy Spirit. If you don't listen to God's insight, you could end up being the problem. Seek to be the solution. Be a rainbow in someone else's cloud!

> For the Lord gives wisdom and from his mouth comes knowledge and understanding. (Proverbs 2:6)

> The fear of the Lord is the beginning of knowledge, but fools despise wisdom and discipline. (Proverbs 1:7)

November 27

Let Your Heart Speak into the Lives of Others

Sometimes you can see someone's cheerful heart through their eyes. You just can't mistake the sparkle, the sincerity, or the kindness and love for anything else. A silent word through a tender smile, especially to a stranger, is like good medicine. You never know when that one smile might be the final push someone needs to say yes to Jesus. God can use you in the process of salvation. Ask the Holy Spirit to guard your heart and mind and make them useful and worthy to fill hearts for Jesus. Let someone see your heart through your eyes.

A cheerful look brings joy to the heart. (Proverbs 15:30)

A cheerful heart is good medicine. (Proverbs 17:22)

November 28

Your Sin can start a Ripple
in Someone Else's Life

Always take responsibility for the effect your actions have had on others. Many times we have suffered because of someone else's sin. You can never be sure how far your sin will reach. Your sin can affect someone else for a lifetime. It's a ripple that sometimes travels into the next generation and even farther. If you know someone who is suffering from your actions, the best thing you can do is to ask for forgiveness from God and the other person. When you've taken care of that, you need to learn to forgive yourself.

> Let your gentleness be evident to all. (Philippians 4:5)

> Make every effort to live in peace with all men and to be holy; without holiness no one sees the Lord. See to it that no one misses the grace of God and that no bitter root grows up to cause trouble and defile many. (Hebrews 12:14)

November 29

People Know What You Stand
For and What You Don't

That feels like an invasion of privacy, doesn't it? Sometimes it seems others know us better than we know ourselves! When we think we are fooling someone else, we are most likely only fooling ourselves and probably not doing much for the relationship. Mixed messages are extremely confusing to others. My favorite friends are those I can trust to be 100 percent truthful with me even if it hurts. Integrity before God should be the same. Although God already knows our thoughts and what we stand for, he still

wants us to come to him in prayer. He wants us to know him through reading his word. He desires for us to call on him day or night because he is the Lord of our lives. It's called a personal relationship, and Jesus died so we could have it. Stand up for Jesus!

> This is the message we have heard from him and declare to you: God is light; in him there is no darkness at all. If we claim to have fellowship with him yet walk in the darkness, we lie and do not live by the truth. But if we walk in the light, as he is in the light, we have fellowship with one another, and the blood of Jesus, his Son, purifies us from all sin. (1 John 1:5–7)

November 30

We Are Responsible for Who We Are and Where We Are Headed

Our childhood circumstances, environment, parents, and family all had a great influence on our lives. But as adults we have a responsibility to work on the areas we are presently in, that are undesirable. We can't continually blame someone else for our situation or failures. We are not eternal victims. No matter how long we have traveled in the wrong direction for whatever reason, we always have the choice to turn around. There is help on every corner for whatever is keeping us from being all that God wants us to be. He's got the best plan. It's our move. It's our life.

> Being confident that he who began a good work in you will carry it on to completion until the day of Christ Jesus. (Philippians 1:6)

December 1

Do You Understand the Concept of God's Love?

At the home of a good friend after the funeral of her young son, I had an opportunity to talk with a group of the young cousins. I believe God

led me to ask if they understood the concept of his love for them. To my surprise, many of them did not but seemed curious, so I prodded a little further. They were asking questions about heaven, so I found a Bible and began to share with them Revelation 21 and 22. Now you may think that book is not child appropriate, but please bear with me. These chapters in Revelation describe the awesome beauty of heaven: its measurements, the atmosphere, the golden streets, God's throne, the pearly gates, and the love of God for all those who enter. Verse 5 in chapter 22 says there will be no more night because God himself will be the light of day. It promises no more crying and no pain. God loves us so much that he created a beautiful place for us to spend eternity with him. The cousins went away with a renewed spirit. They had a better understanding of God's love and were excited knowing they would see their cousin again someday. It was a blessed day all around and totally a God thing. I love when that happens!

> God so loved that world that he gave his one and only Son, that whoever believes in him shall not perish but have eternal life. (John 3:16)

> In my Father's house are many rooms; if it were not so, I would have told you. I am going there to prepare a place for you. (John 14:2–3)

December 2

You can Dream about Great Accomplishments Or Stay Awake and make them Happen

Unless God is speaking to you in a dream, most of them don't mean much. What good is a dream about great accomplishments unless you act on them? Most people don't even remember their dreams, right? So it's probably best if we just listen while we are awake and expect God to put great ideas into our head. He will not leave our questions unanswered. He works through others, circumstances, his Holy Spirit, and the Bible. He will never lead you into something without helping you finish. He has a specific plan for your life, but God has nothing worth having that is easy. He chooses the terms of the gifts he gives us. Trust in him alone.

My sheep listen to my voice; I know them and they follow me. (John 10:27)

Find rest, O my soul, in God alone; my hope comes from him. (Psalm 62:5)

December 3

God Often Opens Wounds to Restore Closed Hearts

Jesus, of course, would be the greatest example of this. Because of Jesus' wounds we are restored to God, but it is up to each of us to receive that truth in our daily living. When you are experiencing a painful, open wound, ask God to show you what he wants you to learn from it. Don't go away empty handed. Maybe you need a change of heart or maybe someone else does. Let God give you the freedom to love. He is the truth, and his purpose is to give life in all its fullness. Be still and know that he is God (Psalm 46:10). Listen, for he is near. Let him speak to your open heart and then wait for the healing.

> Search me, O God, and know my heart; test me and know my anxious thoughts. See if there is any offensive way in me, and lead me in the way everlasting. (Psalm 139:23–24)

December 4

Things Are Often Not as They Appear

God created the earth out of what was not visible. Noah obeyed God and built an ark even though it had never rained before. A closed door often gives way to an open window, and sometimes a no becomes a sudden yes. A mirage has fooled many a wise man. Just because Jesus died on the cross doesn't mean he wasn't the most powerful and influential man who ever walked the earth. Even though you don't feel his presence doesn't mean he's not there. No light at the end of the tunnel doesn't necessarily mean there's no way out. I love how God makes us use our faith to strengthen

us. Have faith and trust in him alone is all he asks of us. Don't lean on your own understanding; it can't hold your weight.

> Now faith is being sure of what we hope for and certain of what we do not see. (Hebrews 11:1)

> So we fix our eyes not on what is seen, but on what is unseen. For what is seen is temporary, but what is unseen is eternal. (2 Corinthians 4:18)

December 5

Our Present Choices Affect Our Future

Do you try to make things happen or do you allow God to move in all circumstances of your life? Do you want more? Do you strive to be in control? Wouldn't it be great to have no regrets at the end of our time on earth? Realistically, that rarely happens. Following the yellow brick road doesn't always lead to the Emerald City. The lion, the tin man, the scarecrow, and Dorothy were all searching in the wrong places for what they thought they needed. There really is no leprechaun sitting with a pot of gold at the end of the rainbow. The truth be told, when we yield all that we have to God, he supplies us with the power of the Holy Spirit. This is the moment we acquire all that we need and our desires become his desires. Choose now to follow Christ and your eternal future will be your inheritance. Oh, the power of the moment!

> Teach me to do your will for you are my God; may your good Spirit lead me on solid ground. (Psalm 143:10)

> Delight thyself in the Lord and he will give you the desires of your heart. (Psalm 37:4)

December 6

Submission Is a Choice to Yield Our Will

"......But as for me and my household, we will serve the Lord" (Joshua 24:15). This scripture is such a true witness of a family living for God. It expresses submission to allow God to work in our lives and to begin and end each day in prayer to know and understand his will. This is a great example to our children to make God a priority in both good times and bad in every aspect of our lives. He has promised to love, protect, and provide for us. Children learn what they live, and if we help them understand the concept of God's love, they will have no problem in following his will for their lives. "Train a child in the way he should go and when he is old he will not turn from it" (Proverbs 22:6). Rather, he will seek it.

> Therefore, do not be foolish but understand what the Lord's will is. (Ephesians 5:17)

December 7

The Blooming Rose on the Other Side of the Garden Wall

Sometimes beauty is in the eye of the beholder. Sometimes it is in the unseen, those things happening behind closed doors. During Jesus' agonizing hours before he went to the cross, he asked his disciples to stay awake awhile and pray. But when Jesus went into the garden of Gethsemane to talk to his Father, they lost sight of him and fell asleep (Matthew 26:40). Because they were asleep on this side of the wall, they did not realize the beauty that was taking place on the other side. The most beautiful and eternal gift from God was about to unfold before the eyes of the world, yet so many, including Jesus' best friends, were spiritually blind to it all. Only those who keep their eyes on Jesus will see and walk on the lighted path. Open our eyes, Lord, so we can see Jesus, and open our ears to hear his call. For what is seen is temporary and what is unseen is eternal (2 Corinthians 4:18).

The man without the Spirit does not accept the things that come from the Spirit of God, for they are foolishness to him, and he cannot understand them, because they are spiritually discerned. (1 Corinthians 2:14)

I was blind, but now I see. (John 9:25)

If a blind man leads a blind man they will both fall into a pit. (Matthew 15:14)

December 8

God Gives Wisdom, Knowledge, and Joy to Those Who Please Him

It's not a difficult undertaking to please the Lord. But when we do, he promises to bless us with the wonders of himself. If you are looking to know God deeper and want wisdom, knowledge, and the joy of the Holy Spirit, it is all at your beck and call. Ask God to fill you with himself. He's the one who gave life to you; it's like he has loaned you your first breath and asks to help you with each continuing breath. You'll breathe easier when you have him in your heart. By standing firm, you will gain life (Luke 21:19).

To the man who pleases him, God gives wisdom, knowledge and happiness, but to the sinner he gives the task of gathering and storing up wealth to hand it over to the one who pleases God. (Ecclesiastes 2:26)

Call to me and I will answer you and tell you great and unsearchable things you do not know. (Jeremiah 33:3)

December 9

To Find Center (Truth) You Must first know the Circumference (God)

It's not always easy to find the center. At times, we tend to stumble over it in the dark. I see the heart as our center because all physical life flows from it. I see God as the circumference because he surrounds us with his presence and all spiritual nourishment comes from him. The heart needs to be in the right place for the truth to be found. I haven't always been aware of God's closeness. I had no idea how big he was! I was walking in the dark and he allowed me to stumble onto the knowledge of his truth. So it wasn't until I found him that I realized my heart had been in the wrong place—a little off center, so to speak. I came out of the darkness into his wonderful light. Don't settle for less than what God wants to give you. His mercies are new every morning. Draw close to him and he will draw close to you (James 4:8).

> Your word is a lamp unto my feet and a light for my path. (Psalm 119:105)

> Create in me a pure heart, O God, and renew a steadfast spirit within me. Do not cast me from your presence or take your Holy Spirit from me. (Psalm 51:10–11)

December 10

God Is Able and Enough

To say that God isn't enough is to say Jesus' death on the cross was insufficient. Would we ask Jesus to do it all over again—and do it a little better next time? When Jesus hung on the cross and said, "It is finished," (John 19:30), he meant that the battle with evil was over. No longer does Satan have control over us in any situation. We have total authority over him, and our best defense is to use it. The Bible says when we look evil straight in the eye and demand it to leave, it will (James 4:7). If you sing praises to God out loud, you will feel God's peace and the absence of evil. God is able and enough! Don't ever doubt that!

But He said to me, "My grace is sufficient for you, for my power is made perfect in weakness." (2 Corinthians 12:8)

Submit yourselves then to God. Resist the devil and he will flee from you. (James 4:7)

December 11

Your Sin Has No Cure but the Blood of Christ

The Bible teaches that being good cannot get you into heaven. Just how good would you have to be? Although God's gift of salvation through Jesus is free, we each must personally accept it. Good works is the *result* of salvation not the *cause* of it. After you've accepted Jesus as your Lord and Savior, his desires will eventually become your desires. Your old habits will be replaced with new ones, and you will no longer have the desire to sin. You will be on God's track, not your own. He will be first and foremost in your life, and you will experience his joy, peace, and freedom. I'm not saying you won't have problems, but now he will go through them with you. He will hold your hand in the dark and lead you where he wants you to go. Think about this: If you could get to heaven on your own, what was Jesus' purpose?

But if we walk in the light, as he is in the light, we have fellowship with one another, and the blood of Jesus, his Son, purifies us from all sin. (1 John 1:7)

For it is by grace you have been saved, through faith—and this not from yourselves, it is the gift of God—not by works, so that no one can boast. (Ephesians 2:8–9)

December 12

What Would God's Love Language Be?

If you haven't read the book, The Five Love Languages, by Gary Chapman, you might consider doing so. He teaches about ~

1) Words of Affirmation (building each other up and showing appreciation)
2) Acts of Service (love in action; doing something to make you feel special)
3) Affection (a warm hug, kiss, touch and sexual intimacy)
4) Quality Time (being together; engaging in an activity you both enjoy)
5) Gifts (giving a gift to show appreciation)

If you know God intimately, you know that he is multilingual. He can speak all five love languages at the same time—fluently! He starts speaking to us before we are even out of bed in the morning. He gives us words of encouragement for the day ahead. He reminds us that he will be with us, participating in our busy schedule. His act of service is his love in action all through the long day and into the night. He follows up in his promises of guidance by the Holy Spirit and gently tucks us in when we lay our head on our pillow at night. And tomorrow when we rise, he will do it all over again. His love is never ending. Listen intently as he speaks.

> And now these three remain; faith, hope and love. But the greatest of these is love. (1 Corinthians 13:13)

December 13

Learn to Love the Sky You are Under

Are you at a time in your life when you really are not particularly fond of your circumstances? Or are you totally content with everything and oblivious to the ever-changing world around you? It is constantly changing; if you feel comfortable now, it won't last forever. It would be unrealistic to think we could ever find utopia here on earth. We can thank Adam and Eve for that. But if we open our eyes and look up and see that the sky is

still blue, just as God created it, we can be thankful for all that surrounds us and know that paradise awaits us. When we see the world through God's eyes, we know this is just our temporary home. Even your present situation is temporary. He knows what you need and already sees the outcome. Strive to live only for today, for it is yours; tomorrow may not be. What color is your sky?

> For I have learned to be content whatever the circumstances. I know what it is to be in need, and I know what it is to have plenty. I have learned the secret of being content in any and every situation whether well fed or hungry, whether living in plenty or in want. I can do everything through him who gives me strength. (Philippians 4:11–13)

December 14

Crown of Thorns, King of Glory

A crown traditionally represents power, victory, honor, and glory. A crown of thorns was placed on Jesus' head during the events leading up to his crucifixion. It was only one of the many barbaric acts of his captors to cause him pain and to mock his claim of authority. Little did the Roman soldiers know that they were fulfilling a prophecy and crowning him as the king of glory for you and for me, and all according to God's perfect plan. If you picture the crown of thorns extending from a beautiful, fragrant bouquet of roses, it portrays how God can take something intensely repugnant and use it for good and for his glory. An utterly awesome thought!

> They stripped him and put a scarlet robe on him, and then twisted together a crown of thorns and set it on his head. They put a staff in his right hand and knelt in front of him and mocked him. "Hail, king of the Jews!" they said. They spit on him and took the staff and struck him on the head again and again. After they had mocked him, they took off the robe and put his own clothes on him. Then they led him away to crucify him. (Matthew 27:28–30)

He said to them, "How foolish you are, and how slow of heart to believe all that the prophets have spoken! Did not the Christ have to suffer these things and then enter his glory?" And beginning with Moses and all the Prophets, he explained to them what was said in all the Scriptures concerning himself. (Luke 24:25–27)

December 15

Doing the Most Good
Happens When You ...

Do all the good you can,
By all the means you can,
In all the ways you can,
In all the places you can,
At all the times you can,
To all the people you can,
As long as ever you can.

-- John Wesley

Let us not become weary in doing good, for at the proper time we will reap a harvest if we do not give up. (Galatians 6:9)

A good man brings good things out of the good stored up in him, and an evil man brings evil things out of the evil stored up in him. (Matthew 12:35)

December 16

Seek the King's Favor (Mercy)

Do you think God is ever disappointed in you? He may stand in wonder at the wrong choices you make, but his mercy is ever upon you. We have his favor through Jesus' death on the cross and his loving-kindness never fails. Please know that his grace can never be taken away from you. If you ask God where you fall short, he will gently show you. Although he loves you just the way you are, he loves you too much to allow you to stay that

way. Be gracious and seek a pure heart. God desires the very best for you. Seek his approval and you will walk in the truth with him by the power of the Holy Spirit.

> He who loves a pure heart and is gracious will have the king for his friend. (Proverbs 22:11)

December 17

Use Whatever Is in Your Hand

Whatever is in your hand or in your control could be a gift from God. On some days the gift is meant for us; on other days it belongs to someone else. But it's been there all along, even when you felt a total lack of God's involvement or concern. If you don't know what your gifts are, ask him and he will show you. Ask him to heighten your awareness of the leading of his Holy Spirit. This is the only way the purpose of God can be fulfilled. God has a specific plan for you. It's hard to grasp things with a clenched fist, but an open hand can receive and also share. Freely you have received, freely give (Matthew 10:8). God chooses the terms of the gifts he gives.

> Each one should use whatever gift he has received to serve others, faithfully administering God's grace in its various forms. (1 Peter 4:10)

> We have different gifts, according to the grace given to each of us. If your gift is prophesying, then prophesy in accordance with your faith; if it is serving, then serve; if it is teaching, then teach; if it is to encourage, then give encouragement; if it is giving, then give generously; if it is to lead, do it diligently; if it is to show mercy, do it cheerfully. (Romans 12:6–8)

December 18

Free People Are Happy People

I have never seen a proud man who was authentically happy, have you? We can't have pride in ourselves and pride in the God we serve at the same time. Those who have excessive self-esteem seem to resist the truth. They can't seem to handle it because it goes against their way of thinking. They limit themselves because they limit God. They see the message of the cross as foolishness instead of the power of God (1 Corinthians 1:18). They are not free to bask in the blessings God wants to grant them. Happy is the man who can draw his love from the heart of the Savior because a cheerful heart has a continuous feast.

> Now the Lord is the Spirit and where the Spirit of the Lord is, there is freedom. (2 Corinthians 3:17)

> For the message of the cross is foolishness to those who are perishing, but to us who are being saved it is the power of God. (1 Corinthians 1:18)

December 19

Let God Settle It While You Are on Your Knees

God is fighting for you. It's his battle, not yours (2 Chronicles 20:15). Even when Jesus was on his knees in the garden of Gethsemane, it was God's battle. Jesus was just the messenger. After you pray, believe your prayer has been answered either in your way or something better. You must be open-minded when talking to God. He may have a purpose for not seeing things your way. If you truly seek him, you will walk away with a sense of peace beyond all understanding. You must believe. God rewards the Christian who seeks him.

According to your faith so be it unto you. (Matthew 9:29)

December 20

Anything Out of Balance
Eventually Breaks Down

Some of the ways God sees things out of balance:

Being unequally yoked together
"Do not be yoked together with unbelievers. For what do righteousness and wickedness have in common? Or what fellowship can light have with darkness?" (2 Corinthians 6:14).

Money
"No one can serve two masters. Either he will hate the one and love the other, or he will be devoted to one and despise the other. You cannot serve both God and money" (Matthew 6:24).

Marriage
"Marriage should be honored by all, and the marriage bed kept pure for God will judge the adulterer and all the sexually immoral" (Hebrews 13:4).

Works
"For it is by grace we are saved, through faith and this is not from yourselves, it is the gift of God—not by works, so that no one can boast" (Ephesians 2:8–9).

Greed
"Then he said to them, 'Watch out! Be on your guard against all kinds of greed; a man's life does not consist in the abundance of his possessions'" (Luke 12:15).

Eating
"So whether you eat or drink or whatever you do, do it all for the glory of God" (1 Corinthians 12:31).

Leadership in the Church
"If it is leadership, let him govern diligently" (Romans 12:8).

All that matters is that I am pure and obedient before God.

December 21

Jesus' Shed Blood Is Everything

Jesus' shed blood broke down all the barriers between God and us. In our long journey to meet him, there may be some potholes, bumps in the road, detours, and even some bridges out, but our arrival is a sure thing. There's nothing left for us to do but accept it. We are stamped "Paid in full. No debt remains." Remember, even if you were the only person on earth, Jesus would have come just for you. He paid the full price in perfect timing, and when he said, "It is finished," he was speaking to all mankind, every tribe, people, and nation. He died as a ransom to set us free. The cross illuminates the word *forgiveness*.

> In him we have redemption through his blood, the forgiveness of sins, in accordance with the riches of God's grace that he lavished on us with all wisdom and understanding. (Ephesians 1:7)

December 22

Is There an Elephant in the Room?

We all have heard about that elephant, as big as life, but everyone pretends it doesn't exist. It represents a truth or problem no one wants to face or talk about. It doesn't belong there, and it's awkward for everyone. It's obviously too big to ignore. If the elephant is never discussed, it will always be there. After one year, five years, ten years down the road, it will have left a stench so awful no one will attempt to go near that room. The elephant might even be forgotten, but the room that could have held your family together can no longer be called a family room. It's just an empty, stinky room with nothing but bad memories. We need to learn to face our problems head-on. This requires hard work, forgiveness, a new perspective, unselfishness, understanding, and possibly open-heart surgery. Open the hearts of the family and bring back a sweet aroma to the home. Engage in heart-to-heart contact.

> Get rid of all bitterness, rage and anger, brawling and slander, along with every form of malice. Be kind and compassionate to

one another, forgiving each other, just as in Christ, God forgave you. (Ephesians 4:31–32)

December 23

Fear of the Unknown

There's a story about a particular room in heaven that holds unsent blessings. The boxes of blessings are beautifully wrapped and tied with huge colored bows and are piled to the ceiling. However, they remain in that room because the person they were intended for was never ready to receive them. Fear of the unknown can freeze you in your tracks and become a real stronghold. To be void of that fear would be to have God's peace. In the book of John, Jesus says he has come to give us his peace (John 14:27). Hopefully, none of those boxes contain the peace Jesus meant for you. Peace moves us forward; fear holds us back. God has an awesome and perfect plan for your life. If you let him lead, you can walk in his footsteps. Walking in the dark with God is far better than walking alone in the light. Grasp his hand and receive his blessings along the way.

> Peace I leave with you, my peace I give you. I do not give to you as the world gives. Do not let your hearts be troubled and do not be afraid. (John 14:27)

> "For I know the plans I have for you," declares the Lord, "plans to prosper you and not to harm you, plans to give you hope and a future. Then you will call upon me and come and pray to me, and I will listen to you. You will seek me and find me when you seek me with all your heart. I will be found by you." (Jeremiah 29:11)

December 24

Unmet Expectations Can Leave Us Empty and Discouraged

Sometimes we need to try to focus on the bigger picture. It's always good to keep things in perspective. God sees things through a totally different

lens. He has promised he will never leave us or forsake us, so when you are facing an obstacle, ask God to show you his purpose in it. It may be for your good or for someone else as a faith builder. When you allow God to enter your life, his grace will always cover you, and his word says his grace is sufficient for you (2 Corinthians 12:9). Jesus' coming has already fulfilled every promise of God. So don't grow weary of doing good (Galatians 6:9). God has nothing worth having that is easy.

> Blessed is the man who perseveres under trial, because when he has stood the test, he will receive the crown of life that God has promised to those that love him. (James 1:12)

December 25

God's Grace

When God gave Moses the Ten Commandments, God knew we would have a hard time keeping them but his intention was that we would depend on him instead of ourselves. Only by his grace can we be saved. We can do nothing by ourselves. Grace nourishes us every day and strengthens and enables us to persevere because God is with us. His power becomes our power through the Holy Spirit. Let God wash you with his grace and mercy, and stop striving to do life on your own. He is the same God who raised Jesus from the dead; certainly he is able to raise you up and show you the way you should go. Be still and know that he is God (Psalm 46:10). His grace is undeserved mercy.

> Whoever gives heed to instruction prospers, and blessed is he who trusts in the Lord. (Proverbs 16:20)
>
> I can do all this through him who gives me strength. (Philippians 4:13)

December 26

Let God Build Your Foundation

A good land developer always contracts with only the very best builders, those who are conscientious about building a sturdy foundation. If the blueprints are not followed precisely, the home will not withstand harsh storms and decay. If we think of ourselves as the home and God as the cornerstone of the foundation, we realize why we might stumble if we disobey his message. We see that our sinful desires (the weak foundation) could war against our souls (our home). Remember, anything out of balance eventually breaks down.

> God's solid foundation stands firm. (2 Timothy 2:19)

December 27

Why We Sometimes Suffer

Suffering shows God's all-sufficient strength and grace much better than if we were exempt of pressure and trial, and makes us more conscious of our dependence on him. It also builds our trust in his leading so we don't dare take a step without him. There is no way to learn faith except by trial. It is better for us to trust God than to enjoy life. Without trust in him, even riches will leave us poor.

> Let us then approach God's throne of grace with confidence, so that we may receive mercy and find grace to help us in our time of need. (Hebrews 4:16)

> Trust in the LORD with all your heart and lean not on your own understanding. (Proverbs 3:5)

> Wait for the LORD; be strong and take heart and wait for the LORD. (Psalm 27:14)

Consider it pure joy, my brothers and sisters, whenever you face trials of many kinds. (James 1:2)

Many are the woes of the wicked, but the LORD's unfailing love surrounds the one who trusts in him. (Psalm 32:10)

Command those who are rich in this present world not to be arrogant nor to put their hope in wealth, which is so uncertain, but to put their hope in God, who richly provides us with everything for our enjoyment. (1 Timothy 6:17)

December 28

God Sometimes Removes Something *in* You before Doing Something *through* You

Sometimes pride or fear can keep you from letting God have the reign of your life. We think so highly or lowly of ourselves that we are determined to change by our own striving. However, a man cannot redeem himself. Redemption is the work of God and is absolutely finished and complete. All wrongdoing is sin. Let his perfect love wash you of your sins. Once you are cleansed, God can use you to serve as Jesus did and build his kingdom— the very reason you were born. If you are wondering what God's will is for you and you do not know what your gift is, your relationship with him might need to go deeper before you can realize his plan.

There are six things the Lord hates, seven that are detestable to him: haughty eyes, a lying tongue, hands that shed innocent blood, a heart that devises wicked schemes, feet that are quick to rush to evil, a false witness who pours out lies and a man who stirs up dissension among brothers. (Proverbs 6:16–19)

December 29

You Can't Want More for Others
Than They Want for Themselves

Have you ever felt burdened for someone you know, to love Jesus and enjoy his peace the way you do? You give them books, invite them to church, and pray for them—and yet you get nothing. Your desire for them to change isn't going to make it happen. Your job is to tell them about Jesus. Tell them how Jesus has affected your life. They need to know and understand that a relationship with God is possible and will bring a new kind of peace. They might even have an idea of what you are talking about, but it needs to travel from their brain to their heart. You plant the seed, and then it's the Holy Spirit's job to water it. When the person finally decides that he or she wants to experience this Jesus, he or she will ask and receive. There's a whole big garden out there ready for harvest. Let the rain fall!

> Ask and it will be given to you; seek and you will find; knock and the door will be opened unto you. For everyone who asks receives; he who seeks finds; and to him who knocks, the door will be opened. (Matthew 7:7–8)

December 30

Don't Settle for a Picnic When
There's a Banquet to go to

I wonder if the disciples, sitting with Jesus at the Last Supper, realized they were attending the most important and prestigious banquet ever and not just joining some friends for a simple, insignificant gathering. Did they realize Jesus was offering himself to the whole world? A banquet so large the King of heaven would be the main event? Did they know they would never hunger or thirst again? Don't settle for less than what God wants to give you. You are an heir; come, feast at his table!

> I am the bread of life. He who comes to me will never go hungry and he who believes in me will never be thirsty again. (John 6:35)

If anyone is thirsty, let him come to me and drink. Whoever believes in me, as the scripture has said, streams of living water will flow from within him. (John 7:37)

December 31

Clouds are a Sign That God Is Still There

The Bible says that Jesus will return to this earth and that his return will be visible for all to see. The most powerful day of all time will be when Jesus comes to gather his loved ones. He will be among the clouds, the very presence of God. It also says that in the end times the weak will leave their faith and follow deceiving spirits. God warns us not to be deceived when antichrists appear and perform signs and miracles to entice us. People believing and looking for direction and comfort from the Universe or anything other than the God who created them are in grave danger of not knowing the truth and being left behind. They miss out on the whole reason of Jesus' birth: salvation and eternity in heaven. Ask God to show you the truth, his absolute truth, and he will. Be ready for that day. Look for the clouds. The Son will be directly behind them!

> The Spirit clearly says that in later times some will abandon the faith and follow deceiving spirits and things taught by demons. (1 Timothy 4:1)

> For many will come in my name claiming, I am the Christ, and many will be deceived. (Matthew 24:5)

> Jesus replied, "But I say to all of you: In the future you will see the Son of Man sitting at the right hand of the Mighty One and coming on the clouds of heaven." (Matthew 26:64)

CPSIA information can be obtained
at www.ICGtesting.com
Printed in the USA
JSHW021526270123
36807JS00002B/7